Growing

RAMONA JONES

Growing

A year of living and nurturing
with the seasons

INTRODUCTION 08

Spring 30

Summer 88

Autumn 142

Winter 200

GARDENING IN A DIFFERENT CLIMATE 246
GLOSSARY 248
INDEX 252
ACKNOWLEDGEMENTS 256

Introduction

These days, if I'm meeting someone new, and it feels safe enough to do so, I'll introduce myself along these lines: 'Hi, I'm Mona. I love gardens, and I'm autistic.'

To most people, those two things probably feel quite separate, and possibly an odd pairing of themes to introduce yourself with. To me, though, they are two core pillars of my identity that feel meshed together in a way that can't be teased apart. In everyday conversation, it's not easy to explain exactly how this works, especially as navigating unrehearsed conversation isn't a strong point of mine.

Over the years, I've found solace in gardening, which has allowed me to discover who I truly am. My grandad introduced me to gardening when I was four years old. The technical term for his land would have been a smallholding, but that doesn't quite capture the magic I felt being in that space as a child. My grandad grew fruit, vegetables and flowers among a collection of animals that changed throughout the years. Sometimes, my sister and I would stay for the weekend and there would be sheep scratching their backs against the apple trees in the orchard. At other times, Grandad would look after goats and ponies when his neighbours went on holiday, and occasionally we would be lucky enough to go for a pony ride around the edge of the garden. Chickens and ducks came and went, and there was always a backdrop of angry geese. The geese were a source of great amusement to my sister and me, and we used to pretend we were musical conductors and wave sticks around them, conducting our 'Goose Opera'.

As a young child, visits to Grandad's garden were simply a pleasure that I didn't think much of. As I grew older, and day to day life (namely school) started to wear me down, Grandad's garden became a place of refuge, where I could build myself back up again.

I have such vivid sensory memories of Grandad's garden that I can take myself right back there in an instant. He had a large greenhouse especially dedicated to growing tomatoes, and through the middle

of the greenhouse was a pathway mulched in broken pieces of terracotta pots. The terracotta would make a satisfying crunching sound as you walked along it. As we watered the tomato plants, the familiar fragrance of the leaves filled the air, sharp and herbal in nature. It's not a universally likeable smell, but in its pungency the scent conveyed a confident reminder that it was summertime, and that I didn't need to worry about those dreaded days at school. My childhood self would marvel at the fuzziness of the tomato leaves as I ran my fingers across their surface, and my shoulders would relax as the warmth of the sun shone through the glass of the greenhouse and onto my skin. The whole process felt like a meditation. I suppose in some sense it was.

Growing up, I continued to find a feeling of escapism in gardens. As a teenager I carefully curated lists of public gardens and green spaces, organised by which month they would be at their peak. Every weekend I would try to check a garden or two off my list. I would take the family dog with me, because his familiar presence made the novelty of a new place less scary. The conventional milestones I was supposed to meet as a young person felt impossible. I had low attendance through school and became very ill with anorexia, and I felt in a constant state of burnout and social overwhelm while trying to attend university. But when I visited those gardens in my spare time, I felt such a deep sense of wonder and magic, and it was just enough to keep me going when the rest of life felt like it was too much.

When I received a late diagnosis of autism, aged 27, I was able to connect the dots on why visiting gardens felt so essential to my well-being. Autistic people can struggle to align themselves with social rules and conventions; we can also be prone to overwhelm from sensory input that non-autistic people can more easily tolerate. School and university felt like a massive melting pot of all the things my autistic brain struggles with – hours of compulsory social time, bright lights, a constant bombardment of information, unwritten social rules, no quiet spaces to hide in. It wore me to the bone, unfortunately in a very literal sense. Public gardens gave me a feeling of resilience in the form of a safe sensory space, a lack of social rules, and a passionate interest (sometimes described as an autistic special interest). They reminded me that I could also feel joy with great intensity. Gardens allowed me to maintain a sense of self when the rest of life was corroding it away.

The autism diagnosis wasn't totally out of the blue, because for my entire life I had a sense that something was unusual. I just didn't have the word to describe my collection of sensory, social and motor difficulties. I couldn't understand why I didn't know my left from right, why I would fall over and walk into things frequently, or why my brain would go totally blank during a conversation that wasn't anticipated. Too much noise or a sudden change of plan could wipe me out for days at a time, and I spent 27 years trying to hide this from other people. Sometimes I would find labels that partially explained my struggles, and I would cling to those in a bid to feel understood. For a while I thought I was at the extreme end of the introversion scale. When I discovered the Myers-Briggs test, which categorises people into one of 16 personality types, I proudly proclaimed my result as an INFJ (introverted, intuitive, feeling, judging) type. INFJs are described as human paradoxes, quiet and peaceful on the outside, but with a deep sense of justice underpinning their decisions. INFJs are known for their ability to mimic others and blend in (a trait that sounds an awful lot like autistic masking). After that, I self-identified as a 'highly sensitive person', which felt like it explained my sensory sensitivities to some extent, but those titles never fitted quite right. Ultimately all of these labels served as decoys that stood in the way of the answer, and nowadays I question their validity altogether.

If I had to summarise what it's like being autistic in a society that isn't accommodating, I would say it wears me down. On the days when I leave the house, I come home feeling heavy and overstimulated at best, and on the verge of meltdown or burnout at worst. Both scenarios are pretty regular occurrences for me, but the key is that they are linked to an unaccommodating society. One thing about being autistic is that we can have intensely passionate interests, and engaging with these is what builds resilience and meaning in our lives. If we are able to tap into these interests in a space that is safe from a sensory perspective, we feel alive again. For me, that's where gardening comes in.

The overlap between getting my own garden and discovering my autistic identity was quite neat. Both events happened within a year of each other. My partner and I had been saving up to buy our first house and, with our budget in mind, I had made peace with satisfying my interest in gardens by visiting public places (in off-peak hours to avoid sensory overwhelm) and buying horticulture books from the second-hand bookshop. But we got really lucky and came across a tiny terraced cottage in Somerset. It was within our budget and it had a very long, thin garden attached to it. Those that had viewed the house before us had avoided buying it on the assumption that the garden was too much work, or that the house was too small. But, for us, it was everything we needed.

After we had moved into the cottage, but before we had any furniture, we propped a laptop up on a cardboard box to watch Netflix. We decided to watch *Atypical*, a series about an autistic boy navigating life in his late teens. A couple of episodes into the series, my partner turned to me and said, 'Isn't it funny how this character has the same difficulties as you, but because he's a man he gets a name for it?' And then the penny dropped. Sure enough, Google confirmed that women can in fact be autistic too, and that the stereotypical picture of autism represented by a white man with difficulty managing social situations and a passion for trains, maths or science (much like the protagonist in *Atypical*) is just one example from a gloriously expansive spectrum of autistic people. So, I joined a lengthy waiting list for an assessment that later confirmed our suspicions.

I had a period in my life where I was learning to garden from scratch while simultaneously unpacking this huge, new piece of information about myself. Both were spiky and unpredictable journeys. Some days felt great, reminding me of my childhood days like when I grew my first tomato in my grandad's garden. Other days felt dull and relentless, like when I began digging out a bamboo plant that had become **invasive** through years of neglect (five years in and I'm still working on removing it all). The same was true of my autism journey. Some days I felt on top of the world with this newly discovered toolkit I could use to help myself – I could take ear plugs on my walks along the road, or wear sunglasses if things were too bright, and my energy would last a bit longer. Other days felt hopeless – I had to confront that my school struggles and eight-year battle with anorexia might have been preventable had people known what I needed as a child. But no matter what I was working through, the garden was always there for me. It was a place where I could learn to unmask without any judgement, and if my mental health felt turbulent, the seasonal rhythm in the garden was a predictable and reassuring constant.

Finding solace in a garden isn't unique to me. Most gardeners have likely had times where their growing space has helped them digest loss, stress or anxiety. Even for those who don't personally garden, visiting a green space can feel like a breath of fresh air in a fast-moving and competitive world, and can help reduce stress for people of all ages.

Through this book I hope to help you nurture your personal journey through the act of gardening, especially for those who are feeling overwhelmed. If you have never gardened before and are feeling intimidated at the thought of getting started, I hope that this book will act as your companion and give you permission to begin.

I have written this book from our garden in the south-west of England. If you are reading from elsewhere in the world, your seasons may look different. Page 247 offers a quick seasonal conversion chart to help you translate my instructions to match your local climate. If any gardening terms are unfamiliar while you are reading, there is a glossary on page 248. Glossary terms are set in bold when they first appear in the text.

Our garden...

... is quite unusual; it is steep, narrow and very long, divided into seven smaller sections. When we moved in, we were informed that the garden measures 300 feet in length and 30 feet in width, but we have never verified these measurements ourselves. Nestled on the slope of a valley, the terrain becomes increasingly steep the further one ventures from the house. This positioning means we lack direct road access, a detail that becomes rather inconvenient when undertaking tasks like building sheds, transporting straw bales and duck food, or hauling bags of **compost**. However, the garden's gradient does grant us a beautiful view from our bathroom window. Through the window, one can see four tiers of the garden at once, each layer merging into the next through a captivating play of perspective. The same holds true for the view from the top of the garden, where multiple layers compress into one detailed image, thanks to the sloping perspective. Standing at the top of the garden in springtime, the bottom of your visual field is filled with layers of delicate bulbs among the grass – daffodils, daisies and snake's head fritillaries. Above, a canopy of white blossoms fills the sky, all framing the backdrop of the cottage itself.

The layers of our garden, starting closest to the house, are as follows:

- Steps and herb garden: the lowest point on the slope. Two flights of stone steps lead from the house to the garden, surrounded by herbs for easy kitchen access. In summer, the steps are softened with masses of *Erigeron karvinskianus* flowers.

- Pond and rose garden: a large smoke tree stands over a wildlife pond (see page 50), home to a thriving newt population. There's a small, flat lawn just big enough for a table and chairs in summer, complemented by a border of pink roses.

- Crocus lawn: our largest flat layer of the garden comprises a mossy lawn with thin borders of hydrangeas and hellebores on either side. The mossy lawn bursts into life with thousands of crocus flowers at the end of winter or early spring.

- Ducks and 'the big greenhouse': here, the lawn becomes more sloping and uneven. On one side, there is a small barn for the ducks and a potting shed. On the other side is a large greenhouse (containing the biggest agave plant I have ever seen), a smaller greenhouse for **seedlings**, and a polytunnel for heat-loving crops.

- Vegetable garden: our vegetable garden consists of seven raised beds, three of which are made from various reclaimed materials – bricks, pallet wood and Victorian path edging. The remaining four are made of railway sleepers (new to us, as reclaimed ones were too expensive).

- Orchard: this area is very hilly and uneven, with grass left almost completely wild. The orchard houses a very large cherry tree, a pear tree, a fig tree, five apple trees, a gooseberry bush and autumn-fruiting raspberry canes that appear in various places.

- Composting and wild area: hidden behind a row of hazel trees is the highest point in our garden, there are three large compost bins and a pond that has been left completely wild. The area is overrun with brambles, and the ground is covered in English ivy.

The garden is more curated close to the house, but as you move up the slope, it becomes wilder, eventually culminating in a 12-foot-tall tangle of brambles at the very top. We are in no hurry to tidy the messy parts of the garden, and I wouldn't have the time or energy to keep it controlled even if I wanted to. In autumn, I enjoy foraging for blackberries among the overgrown brambles, and we've noticed that the local wildlife thrives in these messier parts too. We have spotted bats, foxes, badgers, pheasants, voles, slow worms and grass snakes in the wilder areas of the garden.

Being built into the edge of the valley, our garden experiences different weather patterns at its lowest and highest parts. Near the house, in the lowest part, it's more sheltered and the temperature is slightly warmer. The ground here is boggy, as water flows down the slope and pools at these lower points. Through trial and error, I've learned that tulip bulbs don't fare well in this damp soil and will never offer their flowers for more than one year, and maintaining the grass through winter is a challenging task. Conversely, our wildlife pond benefits from this environment, maintaining a good water level thanks to the constant top-ups from flowing water. At the garden's highest point, conditions are markedly different. It is more exposed, so there's more frost in winter, and any strong gusts of wind cause the most damage here. During summer, this upper part of the garden enjoys the last few hours of sunlight each day. That's where I can often be found, with a book and a blanket, making the most of the long evenings.

A year of observation

We are in our fifth year of gardening now, and I still consider us to be at the start of our journey. There will always be a process of learning through trial and error. Every gardener I have met has told me there is no end to this journey, and that is something that fills me with immense excitement. On the one hand, there is a comforting stability in the seasons; aligning yourself with the movements of nature gives you a gentle momentum that carries you through each year. The darkest days of winter are only ever a part of the transition towards spring. This aspect of gardening feels rhythmic and predictable. On the other hand, though, there is an expansive world of discovery that can lead you to completely different places every year. I've spent a couple of years being entirely fascinated by tulips and crocuses, but I have yet to learn much about trees, fungi, mosses or butterflies. I am currently obsessed with plants that grow from bulbs, but I couldn't tell you what I will be obsessed with this time next year. This part of gardening feels infinite and unknown. In this sense, gardening is an ongoing process of learning that can span across years or, if we are lucky, an entire lifetime. Despite the flashy before and after transformations we watch and share on social media, there is no rush.

It took us at least a year of living here before we really started planting the garden. In part, this was because we were busy and didn't have a lot of disposable income after moving in. In hindsight, though, I would recommend a slow and observant introduction to new gardeners or allotment holders in order to get a good lay of the land. It's especially worth watching through spring and summer, to see what plants emerge through the soil after a winter of lying dormant. My mother-in-law and I learned this the hard way when we started work on her new allotment together in 2018. We were so excited to get started, we completely ripped through any life in the existing beds to make room for new seedlings. We later discovered that, in the process of clearing a bed to plant some young asparagus crowns, we had completely demolished an existing collection of mature asparagus plants. For those who haven't grown asparagus before, the newly planted crowns should be left untouched for two to three years before you can harvest them, so this really taught us both a lesson on slowing down.

During our first year in the garden here, we watched in anticipation to see what would appear through the soil. Surprisingly, it was very little indeed. We were lucky to have a number of mature shrubs and trees, including oak, elder, cherry, hazel, a smoke tree and some palms. But when it came to **perennials** and bulbs, there was next to nothing here. Most of the borders had been kept expertly weeded but completely unfilled. We identified some plants that had become invasive and needed removing or controlling, the worst of which was a bamboo plant

covering an area about 9m (30ft) long. There was also a bed of crocosmia corms that had become overrun through years of abandonment. The corms were so densely populated that I could barely get a fork to pierce the ground when I tried to dig them out. The wildlife pond was full to the brim of yellow flag iris that had also become invasive. I bought a pair of waders and removed three green waste bins' worth of rhizomes by hand in the first year, but by the time the second year rolled around, the remaining rhizomes had multiplied and taken over the cleared space once again. We had to call in backup in the form of two strong men and a pulley system. They pulled out a clump of rhizomes about the size of a large motorbike.

Most of that first year was spent clearing out invasive plants and rebuilding collapsing sheds and garden structures. But there was also time to notice details like weather patterns, wildlife activity and soil health across the garden too. I noticed how the light moves around the garden throughout the day, how some areas nearer the house had heavy clay soil and parts near the top of the garden were of a beautiful loamy texture. I sat on the step of the greenhouse and drank a lot of tea while I watched the world around me. I had time to see where the frost pockets were in winter, and I tried my hand at sowing a few seeds directly into the ground just to see what would happen. There were times when I felt silly for my lack of knowledge or the fact that I hadn't had any formal training, but the garden was teaching me exactly what it could provide and what it needed from me.

When we started adding plants to the borders, I always did so in dribs and drabs rather than in one big transformative push. I like the way this gives me time to watch the garden and ask questions – *what does well in this area and why? What isn't doing well? Which colours of flowers and foliage look good together? Are there times of the year when the border looks weaker, and what can I plant to change this? How have my tastes changed this year?*

If we allow ourselves to surrender to watching the garden, instead of always trying to control it, we can learn so much. This 'dribs and drabs' methodology, albeit a little chaotic, creates so much meaning. I can look at individual plants and remember the reason for adding them, as well as the trip my partner and I took to the garden centre to find them.

Sometimes a particular place will inspire me to plant something. Some of my absolute favourite gardens to visit are in Wiltshire. A visit to Iford Manor inspired me to grow woodland anemones and bluebells in the grass under our oak tree, and the incredible hellebore collection at The Courts Garden made me feel so alive on a grey February afternoon that I wanted to emulate this feeling in my own garden at home. A garden might look beautiful on a surface level to a visiting onlooker, but to the person who planted the garden there is a hidden richness of inspiration from loved ones, favourite places, and months of observation and care.

Something that has stayed with me since our first year in the garden is that although a lot of things in the space were technically messy or wrong, I was just so happy to be there. I didn't know what I was 'supposed' to change in order to have a 'good' garden, and the fact that this didn't hugely matter to my happiness felt very freeing. As I began to share my garden journey online, people would offer traditional gardening advice such as 'your lawn is too mossy', 'it isn't attractive to have a wall covered in ivy', 'you need to weed the dandelions from your lawn', 'keep the grass short', and so on. But when you ask people why we need to do these things, oftentimes they can't answer beyond tidiness. Sometimes, leaving these weeds in place provides food or shelter for insects. My mossy lawn might look uneven, but I see it as a tapestry of interesting colours and textures that exists here for a reason. Moss allows the soil to maintain healthy levels of moisture, absorbs carbon dioxide, increases biodiversity and doesn't need mowing. If it does all these fantastic things and exists here with no effort on my part, why would I spend time removing it and replacing it with something that may not thrive in this environment? This isn't to say that all traditional gardening advice is useless; there is certainly a balance we can aim for. But I have definitely learned that I don't need to care as much about being tidy as I previously aspired to.

Principles of how I garden

Through the last five years of tending to the garden, following and talking with other gardeners, chatting with neighbours over the fence, and attending the occasional lecture here and there, I have developed a gardening methodology of sorts. My garden is a place where I typically enjoy time to myself as an antidote to a busy outside world. However, it's important to reflect on how the garden knowledge that I hold has been shared with me by a variety of voices and experiences. This includes my grandad, my next-door neighbour, whoever has graced our television screen when we've been watching *Gardeners' World* on a Friday night, and the garden content creators and writers I follow online. Even though I may be gardening by myself, the process has been shaped through years of shared experiences and learning, and there is a huge sense of community in this knowledge. Some of the most prominent lessons I've learned are:

Healthy soil is the foundation of a flourishing garden

Conventional gardening advice often suggests that gardeners should dig compost or well-rotted manure into the soil to add nutrients before or after cropping, and to remove weeds by digging. However, I largely adhere to a **no-dig** approach in my garden. This means I keep digging to an absolute minimum and add an annual mulch to the soil surface to build up nutrients and maintain moisture. I use various mulches, including homemade compost, grass clippings, semi-composted duck waste, fallen leaves, or, as a last resort, shop-bought compost. The mulch deprives any weed seeds of light, preventing them from germinating or growing. It is gradually broken down into the soil, supplying nutrients for future crops and flowers. This no-dig approach preserves underground fungal networks and soil organisms, maintaining the soil's healthy structure. The homemade mulches I use become available at random intervals throughout the year, making my **mulching** schedule quite imprecise. I aim to apply one large mulch in autumn-winter, supplemented with grass clippings and other **organic** materials throughout the year.

Grow in polycultures because there is resilience in diversity

We are becoming increasingly aware, through our large-scale food systems, that monocropping has detrimental consequences for soil health, crop resilience and biodiversity. This is also true on a smaller scale in our gardens. **Polyculture**, the opposite approach, involves growing different types of plants together at the same time, mirroring what we observe in the natural environment. Polyculture is a long-established growing technique, rooted in the wisdom of indigenous communities around the world. The cottage garden style that I follow, being a delightful jumble of multiple plants, lends itself quite naturally to polycultures. For example, in my polytunnel, I have spaced permanent edible plants every metre or two, including a dwarf cherry tree, a pomegranate bush, a goji berry bush, and a lemon tree. These permanent residents provide the polytunnel with a stable root structure, maintaining soil integrity and preserving the underground fungal network as **annual** crops come and go around them. I plant annual crops such as chard, kale, tomatoes, cucumbers, and squashes somewhat randomly around the perennials. This ensures there isn't too much competition for specific nutrients in one area and helps to disperse and confuse pests. Then, I intersperse flowers and herbs, including marigolds, chives, basil, parsley, and forget-me-nots, in the gaps among these crops. These smaller plants serve various functions: they attract pollinators, repel pests, add beauty, and provide garnishes for the kitchen. While it may sound quite prescriptive when written down, in the garden, it presents itself as a colourful, muddled and wonderfully surprising array.

You don't need to follow every piece of advice

It may seem contradictory to write this within a list of gardening advice. Gardening encompasses multiple schools of thought, and sometimes ideas on a single topic can completely contradict each other. When someone gives me gardening advice, I ask myself, 'Does this serve my needs?' and 'Does this serve the natural environment?' To use my mossy lawn as an example, several people online have been offended by the moss in my lawn and have recommended that I remove it with a rake, then reseed the exposed soil with grass seed. However, I lack the time, energy and desire to do so, and once I'd learned about the benefits of moss as an insect habitat, a carbon sink and a moisture-retaining layer, the decision became clear for me. There is a collection of traditional gardening advice that follows this same vein, with the overall aim of tidiness, often at the cost of the gardener's time or to life within the natural environment. You have the freedom to decide what holds value in your garden and what deserves your energy. Personally, I find a balance; I'd rather spend an hour tidying the garden followed by an hour enjoying it with a cup of tea in hand, than two hours meticulously grooming every corner.

Learn to love mistakes

In modern life, it's rare to view mistakes positively, but the garden is a very forgiving place. Gardening is inherently a process of give and take between your efforts and external factors such as weather, soil composition or the presence of pests. This dynamic inevitably involves some trial and error. Certainly, some mistakes carry more weight than others; building a shed only to discover that the site is too exposed and the wind has torn it down is far more frustrating than losing a tray of seedlings due to overwatering. However, those smaller, more digestible mistakes can bring us valuable knowledge, and our future attempts become better informed and more attuned to our environment. Through making mistakes, I have learned so much about my growing space and how to operate within it, and I am now more accepting of mistakes in life outside of the garden.

Tread lightly

The impact of our gardening practices extends far beyond our own gardens, and I try to keep this in mind when making decisions and purchases. This will look different for everyone. Some of the ways I try to minimise the wider impact of my garden include making my own compost and mulch where possible, reusing seed trays and pots until they have absolutely no life left in them, using food packaging to make seed labels, and making most of my garden purchases at my local plant nursery and farm shop. I don't aim to be self-sufficient from the food we grow in our garden, but my love of growing tomatoes, chard, herbs and garlic means there are some things we no longer need to buy at the supermarket.

P R S

I

ING

Spring is a time of reawakening.

As the days grow longer and warmer, there is a return of life and colour to the garden, improving day by day. The rewards of autumn and winter bulb planting make themselves known, as the colourful blooms of thousands of crocuses adorn the lawn. I have planted my garden so that the earliest spring blooms can be seen from the window within the comfort of the house. This means that even on colder days, when the thought of being outside isn't as alluring, I can still make it to the window to admire the view. That in itself makes me feel better, and often the act of watching plants through the window is enough to tempt me out of the house and into the garden. And once I'm outside, I am reminded of just how important it is to be there.

Feathered friends

As I walk up the length of the garden I pay a visit to the ducks, who, having weathered the winter 'flockdown', have regained their energy and resumed laying eggs. It has become tradition in our house to celebrate the arrival of spring with a cooked breakfast. My partner Aaron likes to make a fried egg sandwich and I make scrambled egg on wholemeal toast. Duck eggs have very large yolks compared to chicken eggs, and they make a rich and creamy scrambled egg. We have cooked breakfasts with the duck eggs most mornings, and any surplus eggs will go into a nice hearty frittata with some homegrown greens at the end of the week.

In the first week of April in our garden, the damson trees that line the length of the garden are decorated with delicate white blossoms, and there is a quiet hum in the air as more pollinators return to the space above. The earliest tulips erupt into solid blocks of red and pink in the flower borders, underplanted with dainty blue forget-me-nots that self-seed happily around the garden. In our first year of living here, I planted hundreds of *Tulipa* 'Van Eijk' bulbs in the borders, knowing they would be likely to reflower year on year. I was

hoping for a soft pink display from the tulips, but to my disappointment they are a hot red colour that I find a bit abrasive. To their credit though, their ability to rebloom every spring and not diminish in size is quite remarkable. I can't bring myself to remove them because it feels wasteful to dig the bulbs out and replace them with a slightly lighter coloured tulip when they return so reliably. So, I am learning to love them. They are a reminder of the start of my garden journey and a nod of acceptance towards things not always going as planned.

Life in the lawn feels very generous as I don't use the lawnmower through spring. Pale yellow primroses appear of their own accord in the grass, and through gaps in walls and steps. Around them are spring flowering plants that I have introduced myself – clusters of snake's head fritillaries, daffodils and woodland anemones. In the orchard, I grow hundreds of pale white daffodils in the grass. They appear before the fruit trees blossom, so there is an extended period of interest in that space. Our **last frost date** in the south-west of England is usually in the middle of March, so by the start of April the first vegetable seeds are germinating on the greenhouse staging with the promise of bountiful summer harvests, and while we wait for them to grow, a backbone of **perennial** vegetables and a supply of overwintered broad-beans, kale and chard carries us through the **hungry gap** of April and May.

March and April build momentum in the warm-up to the grand finale of May. May in our garden is completely fantastic and bursting with life. On a semi-shaded stone wall next to our cottage, I planted a *Clematis montana*, which is covered in hundreds of pastel pink blooms in the first week of May. I love the combination of a crumbly old wall of mismatched stone being coated in an eruption of perfect fresh flowers. The unmown lawn fills with clover, daisies and soft, billowy cow parsley, all much appreciated by the resident insects. The flower borders, which were previously low-lying, build up to towering heights of white alliums and peonies, lilac irises and soft pink spires of linaria. The colour palette as a whole is pearly and iridescent, best viewed in the hour before sunset.

Climbing plants

Edible plants In the vegetable garden, the asparagus spears are ready to harvest, chives are topped with purple blooms like tiny fireworks, and the perennial onions send up fresh green shoots that we harvest and use in place of spring onions. We planted these in the summer, when I built my perennial vegetable garden from scratch. Last but not least, at the top of the garden, the orchard is filled with pink and white apple and pear blossom in its highest layer, and a mass of cow parsley underneath. If there is ever a time to sit and observe the wonders of the garden, it is now.

Finding glimmers

My morning routine in the early days of spring is one of my favourite things. Each day, I rush to the window after waking up and admire the swathes of purple, white and yellow crocuses. Seeing such vibrant colours after the desaturation of February is my version of a morning cup of coffee. It gives me a boost of energy and I can feel my brain coming back online after the slowness of winter. If it's sunny, the crocus petals unfurl to reveal bright orange stamens, topped with pollen-coated anthers.

The early bees will make their way across the flowers as they feed, rolling around in the centre. Sometimes they stay nestled in the petals to rest. Bumblebees and honeybees have pollen pockets, also known as corbiculae, on their hind legs. As they move from flower to flower, you can watch them fill their pockets until it looks like they are wearing a tiny orange pair of pollen trousers. I planted the crocuses mainly because I love seeing bright colours early in the year, but watching the bees and other pollinators as they utilise the flowers has become a seasonal ritual for me, and I look forward to it every year.

These moments of intense sensory joy are known within the autistic community as glimmers. A glimmer is the opposite of a trigger – it is something that calms and relaxes a person, or offers them joy, and helps them to reregulate their nervous system. Before my partner and I came across the term glimmer, we would describe the phenomenon as 'brain fireworks'. One afternoon we were walking through a park together and we noticed a clump of a few hundred crocuses flowering under a tree. They shone brilliantly against the well-trodden mud of the football pitch, and I couldn't take my eyes off them. I told my partner that I could feel my brain recharging while I was staring at them, and he lovingly coined the phrase 'brain fireworks'. Now that I know a lot more about how the autistic brain works and what it needs, I realise that these moments are glimmers, and I try to facilitate as many as I possibly can in my own garden.

Many autistic people, including myself, are detail-oriented. We notice tiny details quite naturally, perhaps at the cost of missing the bigger picture. I sometimes describe my experience of the world as though I'm looking through a telescope – it's like I can only see one part of a scene at a time, in great detail, while most other people are able to take in a sweeping view of the entire scene. I need to move slowly through all parts of the scene to take it in, and if that process is rushed (as it often is in our modern way of life) I can end up overwhelmed.

This is the process by which life overwhelms me, but it is also the process that allows me to experience intense joy through glimmers. To be in the midst of a glimmer feels safe and blissful. It is like all background noise and stressors fade away, and your mind is entirely consumed by one object of beauty and fascination. Once we know the specific images, colours, sounds or patterns that bring on glimmers, we can seek them out and look for them more often as a gesture of care towards ourselves. The bright colours of spring bulbs appear especially vibrant when we have been without them for so long in the months prior, so spring feels especially rich in sensory glimmers.

Leaning into the smaller details in our gardens or local green spaces is something that can bring relief for a great number of us, regardless of our neurotype. We are living in a time where work tasks and social media apps are constantly fighting for our attention, and through their immediacy and persistence we can neglect the simple details around us to the detriment of our mental health. For those whose brains can scan an entire scene, perhaps there is a sense of sanctuary to be found in zooming in on the smaller parts of that scene?

To lean into experiencing glimmers in your own growing space, spend some time noticing the small things that bring you a sense of relief. Perhaps you already know what your favourite flower or plant is – what are the parts of it you like? Does it change with the weather? Maybe there is magic in the way the sunlight shines through the petals and illuminates the colours in the morning. It might be that glimmers for you are more tactile, like the way warmth of the sun lands on the surface of your skin, or a cold breeze bringing you a sense of freshness on a windy day. The more you start to notice small pleasures like these, the more you will find.

As you start to identify these glimmers, make space for them in your garden and find the time to engage with them without distraction. For me this looked like planting thousands of crocus bulbs among the grass, and having my morning cup of tea among them in spring when the weather permits. Be sure to notice how spending time with these plants makes you feel. After I have spent half an hour watching bees on the crocuses, I usually feel inspired and excited. There are other glimmers in the garden that bring me a different set of positive emotions. Water is one for me – I might sit and watch reflections on the pond, observe the morning dew on the lawn, or watch water droplets roll down the surface of my vegetable plants after I have watered them. Water makes me feel calm and (rather fittingly) reflective. Our gardens give us a space where we can curate a world full of glimmers, and when we give them our time and attention we will be rewarded with a host of positive sensations and emotions.

Embracing an untamed lawn

We have participated in what in the UK we call 'No Mow May' every year since we moved into our cottage, at least to some extent. No Mow May involves leaving lawns to grow naturally throughout late spring, in turn fostering the growth of **native** wildflowers and providing a haven for insects. This initiative was created by the British conservation charity Plantlife in 2019, but has since gained international traction.

The UK has witnessed the loss of 97 per cent of its flower-rich meadows since the 1930s. This dramatic decline not only represents a loss of beauty but also signifies a loss of vital food sources for pollinators. Numerous moth and butterfly species are in decline due to the loss of their natural habitats, leaving them with fewer places to nest, breed and forage. Flower-rich meadows also act as carbon sinks, playing a crucial role in mitigating the impacts of climate change, so the No-Mow movement aims to redress this imbalance by encouraging the rewilding of people's gardens. A month teeming with floral and pollinator activity is an ideal time to embrace an untamed lawn.

With this being our first home, we didn't own much in the way of furniture or tools when we moved in, lawnmower included. I took my time trying to find a lawnmower that was light enough for me to carry up between the terraced levels of our garden, and the first few weeks of May escaped me in that process. Then I came across No Mow May, and thought we had nothing to lose – and the energy saved in not mowing was appealing in its own right.

Because we didn't mow at all in that first attempt, not even a path through the long grass, the garden was very wild and difficult to navigate, especially for the dogs. Since then we have reached a compromise whereby we mow paths for access, some areas of short grass for the dogs and ducks to use, and then we leave about half of the garden completely wild for at least a month. Keeping some paths and short areas is helpful for retaining some sense of tidiness among the wild, which my inner perfectionist appreciates.

Different parts of the garden behave in different ways through late spring. The grass closer to the house becomes full of clover, common daisies, wild violets, creeping buttercups and ox-eye daisies. The flowers of these plants are like beautiful tiny embellishments dotted through the rich green grass. At the top of the garden there tend to be more taproot flowers like dandelions, cow parsley, comfrey and borage. My dad has been lucky enough to find bee orchids flowering in his lawn at the start of June after a break in mowing, though we have yet to see any wild orchids here. Despite their differing flowers, all areas of our garden have in common that they are filled with bees, flies, beetles, birds and other creatures when we stop mowing. Allowing the lawn to grow long also benefits our **naturalised** spring bulbs like crocuses and snake's head fritillaries, giving them time to photosynthesise after flowering and replenish their energy for next year's blooms.

Soil health

Watching the flowers (or weeds) during this time of year gives us information about the soil, and nature's efforts to reinstate a balance. Deeper taproots, like those of the dandelions and cow parsley at the top of our garden, indicate compacted soil with fewer surface nutrients. Through the complete the lifecycle of the weed, the root loosens compacted earth around it and pulls nutrients from deeper levels, returning these to the top layer of the soil once the weed has died and composted. Those of us who make organic fertiliser with comfrey leaves are taking advantage of this same process, taking nutrients from the soil via deep taproots and composting the foliage to disperse these nutrients across the top layer of soil in the vegetable patch.

Make friends with your weeds

Seeing weeds in the grass, and the wildlife presence that accompanies them, makes me wonder why we demonise them so much to begin with. Of course, they can be a nuisance when they compete with our prized crops, and they may swamp the curated parts of our gardens if we don't step in at all. But there is definitely a middle ground somewhere between a perfectly tidied garden and a fully wild one.

You may wonder, though, what's the point if you're going to mow it all down again in June? For those who choose to give up mowing and provide forage for pollinators for one month, it's much better than nothing at all. Beyond that, the No-Mow movement sparks useful conversations and learnings that we can take with us through the whole year. We are confronted with the sad reality of the decline of wild habitats around our homes, but we are also presented with the power of being able to do something about that in our gardens and allotments, or by encouraging our local councils and farmers to mow less and rewild more. We learn that weeds can be beautiful and beneficial, and we should let a few more of them in – and that it isn't the end of the world for our garden to look a bit messy. More and more of us are reflecting on what we can do for pollinators the rest of the year: choosing to avoid weed-killers and pesticides to protect wildlife, mowing less year-round, building bug hotels and hibernation spots for overwintering insects (see page 177), and planting flower borders with pollinators in mind.

Our wildlife pond

Ponds are hugely valuable resources for wildlife in a garden. Even the smallest of ponds can support a vast collection of creatures, including frogs, newts, water snails, dragonflies, damselflies and water beetles, to name a few. The species that live in and around our ponds support the wider ecosystem in the garden as well. We have a beautiful population of pipistrelle bats in our garden, and after sunset, these bats feast on the flies that spend their larval stages in the water.

In the spring and summer, we observe a number of birds bathing in the pond or drinking from it. This year, we have a pair of collared doves that meet up throughout the day at the edge of the pond, paddling in the

shallow end and having a drink before going their separate ways again. If our dogs are patrolling the garden, the doves will wait patiently in the smoke bush foliage above until the coast is clear and they can return to the water.

We have two medium-sized ponds in our garden, one at the very bottom and one at the very top. Both are around 2.5m (8ft) wide, and 1m (3ft) deep in the centre. Thankfully, these ponds were here when we moved in, so we didn't have to do any hard work digging. We did have to empty, drain and re-line them, though, as they had become completely overrun with invasive yellow flag iris, and the pond liner had torn and started leaking where the iris roots had broken through it. After we had repaired the liner and refilled the pond, we noticed wildlife taking to the area in a surprisingly short amount of time. Within a month, there were new frogs, dragonflies and beetles on the surface of the water, not to mention the life that had likely returned beyond what was visible to us from the lawn.

I am planting our pond gradually, and while it is not yet completely planted up, I have introduced some oxygenating pond weed in the water, a few marginal plants including Siberian iris (*Iris sibirica*), water forget-me-nots (*Myosotis scorpioides*) and water mint (*Mentha aquatica*), and I am currently searching for a suitable water lily.

It is very much worth adding a pond to your growing area for the value it brings to the garden ecosystem and the subsequent pest control gained through this natural food chain, even if the pond is only small. I grow hostas around the edge of our pond, plants that are notorious for their tendency to be eaten by slugs and snails. Thanks to the frog and newt populations that feed on slugs, damage to our hosta plants is kept to a minimum.

CREATING A POND

❧ A small, watertight container is an excellent way to create a pond in your garden with minimal effort and cost. Begin by selecting a sturdy container such as a half whiskey barrel, large planter or any other large, watertight vessel. Ensure it has no leaks and is safe for wildlife.

❧ Place your container in a spot that receives a balance of sunlight and shade, as too much sun can lead to algae growth, while too much shade can limit plant growth.

❧ Clean the container thoroughly to remove any residues and, if necessary, line it with a pond liner to ensure it is completely watertight. Fill the container with water, preferably rainwater, as tap water can contain chemicals harmful to aquatic life. Let the water sit for a day or two to reach ambient temperature and allow chlorine to dissipate.

❧ After the water has sat for a couple of days, introduce a mix of oxygenating plants, marginal plants and floating plants, such as water lilies, water hyacinth, duckweed and oxygenating plants like hornwort, which will help keep the water clean and provide habitat for wildlife.

❧ Regularly check the water level, topping up with rainwater as needed, and remove any dead plant material while controlling algae growth by adding more oxygenating plants or using a barley straw extract.

By following these steps, you can create a thriving mini-ecosystem that will attract various forms of wildlife and enhance the biodiversity of your garden.

Spring seed sowing

Spring is a wonderful time to learn about seed sowing if it's something you've not tried before, safe from the cold of winter and with lengthening daylight hours. You'll notice the process happening naturally around your growing space too, as self-sown weeds or wildflowers sprout from bare soil. I always look forward to sowing a big batch of seeds in April. Seed trays full of fresh compost are like a blank canvas, with the promise of creating kilograms of delicious food come summer. The fact that something so tiny as a seed can hold the potential to become a tray of orange and crimson tomatoes that I will roast in olive oil for dinner, or a mighty pumpkin that we will carve for Halloween, never fails to amaze me.

Edible plants   I used to look at my grandad's greenhouse and wonder why he filled it exclusively with tomato plants. Now that I have some experience of growing my own food and flowers, though, I completely understand the allure of tomatoes. If I had to choose just one plant to grow, I would most likely choose the same. I grow mostly edible plants from seed, and the occasional annual flower such as cosmos or aster, to pad out the borders with something beautiful or to entice pollinators into the garden. This is a personal preference rather than being the 'right' way to grow seeds. The beauty of growing your own food and flowers is in exploring different varieties and learning what does well for you and what you find the most rewarding.

Most years, I will try growing a couple of new things to see if they feel worthwhile or if I can handle the challenge of novelty. But I have completely fallen in love with the process of growing food, and I find enough beauty within the flowers of a pea vine or tomato plant, and the subsequent produce that follows, that I haven't felt a strong pull towards growing annual flowers. I also grow lots of perennial flowers in my borders, and I find these to be just as wonderful and much lower maintenance than annual flowers. So, I am first and foremost an edible seed grower.

HOW TO SOW

❦ I almost never sow directly into the soil (unless the seed is for a root vegetable like carrots or parsnips), instead using seed trays or **modules** filled with a mix of compost and **vermiculite**. Vermiculite helps with moisture retention and aeration, which can aid seedling development. Sowing in modules and trays helps me to avoid slug and mouse damage to vulnerable young plants. The main reason I don't sow directly into the soil, though, is that I grow my crops in a happy muddle among perennial vegetables; it is easier for me to slot smaller plants into my scheme than it is to raise tiny seedlings around established plants. I also love the sense of purpose and wonder I feel when I can lift the trays up and inspect the new life within those tiny seedlings. Growing some trays on a windowsill in the house helps me bring these feelings indoors.

❦ I sow most of my seeds in an unheated but sheltered spot, usually in my shed next to the window or on staging in the greenhouse. My greenhouse has a **deciduous** tree growing over it, so there is maximum light in the spring while the tree is bare, but in summer the leaves help to provide some dappled shade and protect my plants from getting singed by harsh sunlight. A cold frame or polytunnel would also work for seed sowing, or if you are starting your seeds indoors, a windowsill or a table next to a window are good options.

❦ There is plenty of guidance available on which size seed tray to use for particular types of seed, which type of compost is best, the ratio of compost to vermiculite and perlite, and so on. Some of this is personal choice, and it is always good to experiment and find the methods that work best for you. I rescue most of my seed modules from the reuse bin in our local garden centre, so I tend to use whatever size modules I have available, and it's served me pretty well so far. Similarly with compost, I try to buy a peat-free multipurpose compost for seed sowing, and mix in a handful of vermiculite when I am filling seed trays, but I haven't yet found one brand of compost that I am particularly loyal to and I am not prescriptive on ratios of vermiculite to compost.

❦ When it comes to sowing seeds, larger seeds like peas or beans will be planted one per module, while smaller seeds can be multi-sown. It's best to check the seed packet for specific requirements including warmth and planting depth, though generally speaking bigger seeds will be planted deeper, and tiny seeds (like poppy or foxgloves) will be pressed onto the surface of the compost. Remember to label your seed trays to avoid confusion. I make my own plant labels with waste food packaging like ice cream tubs or milk cartons, and write on these with a permanent pen.

❦ When it comes to watering, I place my seed modules in larger plastic trays, and then I fill these trays with water so that the compost in the seed trays can soak up the water from underneath. This method disturbs the compost less than overhead watering, and I also find it easier than using a watering can because I am quite clumsy and uncoordinated. When the compost looks or feels dry to touch, or if the plants are looking a bit dry or curled over, it's a good time to top up the water trays.

❧ Sedlings will produce one set of generic-looking round leaves before producing a set of **true leaves**. True leaves resemble tiny versions of the adult plant. Once my seedlings develop true leaves, I remove any that look weaker or unhealthy (this is known as **thinning out**). I also **prick them out** and transplant the young plants into a slightly larger pot at this stage (though not one that's excessively large). This process, known as **potting on**, ensures the young plants receive adequate nutrients and grow robust enough to withstand being planted in the garden. If I was to place these seedlings directly into the garden, they might be too fragile and vulnerable to pests, harsh weather conditions or competition with other roots in the soil.

❧ I make it a point to pot on the seedlings I particularly care about or those that are more demanding, like tomatoes and aubergines. However, there are times when I'm busy or tired, and the occasional tray of chard or kale is left to outgrow its seed modules before being directly transferred into the soil in the polytunnel. Life can get in the way, and I've learned that some plants don't require as much pampering as others.

❦ If you have started your seedlings in a sheltered location such as a windowsill or greenhouse and plan to transplant them into the garden, it's crucial to acclimatise them to the outdoor weather conditions before planting them out in the open. This is especially important if they have been raised in your home, benefiting from constant heating, as the nights are much colder outdoors, and the plants need to gradually adjust to this change. This gradual acclimatisation process is known as **hardening off**.

❦ To harden my seedlings off, I begin by moving them closer to the greenhouse door, gradually increasing the time the door is left open over a span of a couple of weeks. However, it's important to note that I only do this for plants whose final position will be in the garden. Most of my crops will be planted in the polytunnel and, therefore, don't require hardening off.

❦ For seedlings started in the house, the best approach to harden them off is to initially move the trays outside to a sheltered spot during the day, then bring them back in at night for about a week. This allows the seedlings to experience a gentler version of the temperature fluctuation they'll face in the garden. During the second and third weeks, you can leave the trays outdoors in the sheltered spot but cover them with fleece at night. The fleece helps protect the young plants from drastic drops in temperature and from potential frost.

❦ Remember, the greater the temperature difference between the seedlings' initial environment and the garden environment, the longer and more gradual the hardening off process should be. This careful transition helps prevent shock, allowing your plants to adjust, strengthen and ultimately thrive in their new outdoor environment.

I think if I had read all of these rules and recommendations when I was starting out on my gardening journey, I would have worried that they were absolute, and that things had to be done in a very particular way in order to grow any food. Keep in mind, though, that the seeds already contain all the information needed to become a flourishing plant. We just need to help them meet their requirements for soil, light and water, and potentially provide some protection from pests and weather too. You may well find that if you throw a packet of beans over your shoulder into the soil, they produce just as good a harvest as that of your neighbour who has meticulously cared for their crop from sowing in the potting shed to finally planting out in the raised bed. So, if you are new to growing, start small, remember the value in learning through mistakes, and don't be afraid of simply giving something a try.

SEED SOWING
CHECKLIST

○ Choose a sowing location with adequate light and protection from harsh weather conditions, such as a cold frame, greenhouse, polytunnel or windowsill.

○ Fill seed trays or modules with an equal mix of compost and vermiculite (or just compost), and gently compress the compost into the tray.

○ Sow your seeds at depths specified on the packet. Larger seeds (e.g. peas or beans) are sown deeper and with more space (one per module), while smaller seeds can be multi-sown on the compost surface. Cover seeds with a fine layer of compost if required. Remember to label your seed trays.

○ Place seed modules in larger plastic trays and fill the trays with water to allow compost to soak from underneath, and top up with water when the compost feels dry to the touch or when plants appear dry.

○ Pot on seedlings into slightly larger pots once true leaves develop, and remove seedlings that look discoloured or stunted.

○ Gradually acclimatise seedlings to outdoor conditions if they were started in a sheltered location. Increase their outdoor exposure over a couple of weeks, covering them with fleece at night to protect from cold.

WHAT AM I SOWING IN SPRING?

Here is a rough guide to what to sow in spring. This guide is based on my garden in the south-west of England (which is the equivalent of a USDA zone 9a). Our last frost date is usually mid-March, but I keep my eyes on the weather forecast in case any seedlings need covering with fleece or moving indoors for a night in the weeks afterwards, just to be super safe. Seeds can be quite forgiving, so don't fret if you are running a few weeks late and still want to sow something; it's still worth doing.

MONTH	FOOD	FLOWERS
● March	· Peas · Broad beans · Lettuce · Spinach · Radishes · Onions · Parsley · Coriander · Dill · Parsnips · Tomatoes (on a heated **propagator**)	· Sweet peas · Marigolds · Calendula · Dianthus
● April (anything from the March sowing list can still be sown)	· Leeks · Chard · Carrots · Beetroots · Tomatoes · Sweetcorn · Melon	· Sunflowers · Nasturtiums · Zinnias · Cosmos · Lupins
● May	· French beans · Climbing beans · Potatoes · Courgettes · Pumpkins · Cucumbers	· Dahlias · Snapdragon · Campanula · Aster

Welcoming new flowers, trees and shrubs

While a visit to the nursery is enjoyable any time of year, and I do introduce plants at intervals throughout the year (when the weather permits), the reassurance and excitement of spring makes it a particularly wonderful time for planting a border.

The warm and moist soil provides a nurturing environment for young roots to establish new growth, while the increasing levels of daylight fuel photosynthesis. Young plants introduced in spring benefit from a full season of warmth, increasing the likelihood of flowering within their first year compared to those planted later. Conversely, introducing plants during the height of summer can be challenging, as high temperatures and dry soil may hinder their establishment. Planting later in the year poses its challenges too, particularly for **tender** plants that require time to establish before the onset of frosts.

Choosing your plants

Selecting plants can initially seem daunting. The pressure to instantly create the perfect space is very real, amplified by the impressive before-and-after videos we see on social media. However, curating your garden is an ongoing labour of love. Even with a significant initial planting effort, it will take years for plants to fully establish and settle into the space. Some plants will flourish, while others may not perform as expected, and that's perfectly fine. Gardening requires patience and attentive observation. My own garden has been planted and topped up in gentle waves as time and money have allowed, and most of our plants were introduced in nine-centimetre pots and given time to grow into their space because it was the most affordable option.

To maintain a sense of motivation while the garden is getting established, consider planting favourites that promise blooms in their first season. For me, roses were the answer. A month before moving into our home, my partner and I chose a selection of our favourite roses for the borders during a visit to the David Austin show garden. Since the roses were already a few years old when we picked them up from

the nursery, we enjoyed blossoms within a few months of planting in our garden, and every year the roses grow and become generous in their flowering. These more instant rewards inspire me to plant things that have a delayed sense of gratification attached to them, like peonies and irises. I've learned to appreciate the beauty in each individual flower, understanding that the bigger picture will unfold with time.

If you are starting a garden from scratch, prioritise planting larger elements like trees, hedges and **topiary** early on. They'll grow slowly in the background, providing structure while you focus on smaller details and fine-tuning.

Watering

Established plants shouldn't need watering at this time of year (unless they are in pots) because they have a deeper root system that can draw moisture from the soil. New plants will need a bit of help with watering during their first year while they establish their roots. When I add a new plant to the garden, I give it a generous drink of water immediately after planting and add a layer of mulch around the base of the plant to help conserve moisture (usually grass clippings, leaf mulch or compost). I keep an eye on the new plants throughout the spring and summer, and if their leaves ever look dry or droopy, I give them water at the base of the plant and top up their mulch.

Wildlife friendly

Research has shown that the most ecologically beneficial gardens grow a mix of native and **non-native** plants. Native plants are those that occur naturally in the area where your garden is located. In my garden in the south-west of England, this includes English oak, primroses, pasqueflowers, foxgloves, dog roses and many other wonderful species. Explore what plants are indigenous to your part of the world. Native plants support local pollinators and wildlife, and they are well-adapted to the local climate and soil conditions. Non-native plants are also beneficial in the garden because they can extend the flowering season and provide sustenance for insect life during times when native plants are less prolific. Crocuses, for example, are not native to the UK; they are indigenous to the Mediterranean, eastern Europe and northwestern China. In my garden, they bloom at the end of February, and as our winters are becoming milder, the crocuses offer a vital food source to pollinators that become active earlier in the year when few other plants are in bloom. A combination of native and non-native plants ensures a longer flowering season, and this diversity allows us to support a broader range of insects more effectively.

When choosing plants, it's essential to check whether a species could be invasive in your area. An invasive plant will spread rapidly and can become difficult to control; it may outcompete other valuable or native plants not only in your garden but also in the surrounding natural landscape. If you're unsure whether a plant is invasive in your region, a quick online search can provide valuable guidance. A large proportion of the first two years in my garden were spent removing species that had become invasive, and this time could have easily been freed up if previous gardeners had been more attentive.

WHAT AM I PLANTING IN SPRING?

My patch of the world exists in a temperate climate and enjoys good sun exposure. For shaded gardens, the selection process will differ. Always verify that a plant isn't considered invasive in your area before planting. Additionally, consider plant toxicity if you have pets or young children.

Trees

My cottage garden is both productive and ornamental, so I look to grow trees that serve a few purposes. Apple trees, for example, not only offer beautiful blossoms in spring, attractive to humans and pollinators alike, but also provide bountiful fruit harvests as summer draws to a close. I grow a mix of apple, cherry and pear trees in the orchard. One of the varieties of apple tree I grow is called 'Red Windsor', which produces a wonderful shiny red dessert apple with a satisfying crunch. I also grow hazel trees at the back of the garden so I can **coppice** the stems and use these to build supporting structures around my vegetable plants – we could potentially harvest hazelnuts from these trees too, but the squirrels always seem to get there before we do.

Along the edges of our garden are about 15 to 20 damson trees of various sizes, self-seeded over the years from discarded stones. Each summer, they provide fruit for jam-making. Many of our damson trees have grown tall in their maturity. Unable to reach their fruit by hand, I have a summer routine of parading up and down the lawn with a basket every few days collecting the fallen ripe fruits for jam. I am not an expert when it comes to making jam, but making damson jam is a forgiving process due to damsons' high pectin content, which holds the jam in a firm texture. The damson trees also offer a lovely display of blossoms in spring, and act as a natural privacy screen in summer. In autumn, the fallen leaves are left to form a natural mulch on the borders, contributing to the soil's fertility. The lifecycle of these trees embodies generosity throughout the entire year.

Be mindful of size when you are selecting trees; some have the potential to grow very large as they mature. In smaller gardens or pots, dwarf rootstock varieties might be more suitable. Trees also offer privacy and structure, or can be trained in unique forms. For compact spaces, consider apple and pear 'stepovers' along border edges. These trees, characterised by a short trunk and two horizontal stems, offer a creative way to grow fruit in limited areas. If you're planting a single fruit tree, ensure it's a **self-fertile** variety. Some trees require cross-pollination to bear fruit, so a self-fertile tree is essential if it's the sole specimen.

I try to grow a selection of fruits that are typically imported, like cherries, nectarines and figs. Harvesting from these trees in summer reduces our food miles, which in turn lowers our carbon footprint. In a broader sense, growing these fruits also attunes us to the seasonal rhythm of food, a lesson that our modern food systems typically deprive us of. The anticipation of fresh figs as summer arrives makes their flavour all the more precious.

Consider these fruit and nut trees for a productive garden: apple, pear, plum, peach, nectarine, apricot, damson, quince, cherry, fig, mulberry, medlar, hazelnut, almond and cobnut.

Hedges and topiary

Topiary is the art of clipping shrubs and trees into ornamental shapes. Neat and symmetrical shapes like domes, spikes or rectangles can add a sense of structure or formality to the garden, while playful shapes such as animals, clouds or abstract forms can introduce a sense of whimsy and amusement. Topiary can also introduce year-round height to borders, especially when plants are trained as standards or 'lollipops'. I am still mastering the art of trimming a shrub into a perfect spherical shape, so although the idea of a topiary animal is appealing, in my garden, I opt for simple structures like domes, balls and lollipops. I love the backbone they provide to the garden, and shaping them in the summer can be a very satisfying process.

Evergreen varieties of hedge or topiary are particularly valuable for bringing life into a winter garden while other plants are dormant. Box and yew are classic choices and can be trained as hedges or into various shapes such as domes, lollipops and balls. Although box looks beautiful once it is established and trained into your shape of choice, fewer people are choosing to plant it nowadays due to the threat of box tree caterpillars. These hungry caterpillars will happily feast through every scrap of foliage on a box hedge until the plant becomes completely devoid of energy, and currently, there aren't any known natural predators to keep the caterpillar population under control. If you are planting from scratch, it's much easier to opt for resistant alternatives to box, for example, *Ilex crenata* (box-leaved holly).

Because our garden is long and thin, I try to curate a sense of continuity throughout its length by repeating some plants and similar shapes along the length of the garden. Topiaries are particularly important for this – each section of the garden has some sort of evergreen topiary clipped into a sphere. The sense of similarity between these repeating plants and shapes pulls distant parts of the garden closer together, and the space feels more unified as a result. If time and energy allow, I trim the topiary twice a year – once at the beginning of summer and once at the end. Sometimes I miss the second trim, but I try to clip them at least once a year so the

shapes are maintained and don't have a chance to grow out. I use a battery-powered hedge cutter to do so, as I find it much faster than trimming with garden shears. It is important to trim hedges with sharp tools, as this will create clean cuts through foliage and minimise the risk of disease.

We inherited some beautiful mature box balls when we moved into our garden. However, in recent years they have been absolutely swamped with box tree caterpillars throughout the summer. I don't like the idea of treating the hedges with a product because I try to encourage natural pest control in the garden, so I am gradually replacing the box with *Ligustrum ovalifolium* (garden privet) lollipops and box-leaved holly balls, which provide evergreen structure without the risk of blight or caterpillar predation. To the untrained eye, it is hard to spot the difference between box and box-leaved holly, and I only wish I had swapped the plants around sooner. In the winter months, I really value having the enduring green topiary structures to admire, and in the summer the formality of a neatly trimmed dome gives me some sense of control while perennials grow wild everywhere else. I like the garden most when human design meets the chaos of nature.

For year-round privacy, evergreen options include privet, yew, bay, box-leaved holly, holly, beech and camellia. These can be shaped into hedges, domes, balls or other structured forms.

If you want something beautiful and useful, consider training bay, rosemary or fig trees as standard plants, giving you a source of food or herbs combined with formal aesthetics.

For biodiversity, consider a mixed-species hedge, providing food and shelter to local wildlife. In the UK, options include hawthorn, blackthorn, hazel, beech, hornbeam and holly, with climbers like wild roses or blackberries offering additional support. Each species contributes uniquely to the ecosystem, so a mix of species can be very beneficial.

Shrubs

Shrubs add structure, height, and can bring a burst of colour to your borders with flowers or colourful autumn foliage. Their sturdy wooden stems can be helpful for creating shape and form around perennials that fluctuate in size throughout the year. Position taller and more substantial shrubs at the back of borders to build up height, while medium-sized shrubs such as roses can be placed in the middle of the border with perennials. As with other types of plants, shrubs need watering in their first year in the garden, as their roots get established.

In the borders around my crocus lawn, I grow an assortment of hydrangeas. After many childhood holidays to Cornwall, I used to think of hydrangeas as plants that belong to coastal gardens only, but they look quite at home in a cottage garden too. Areas of our borders are in **partial shade**, and the hydrangeas tolerate this quite well, still flowering for a long period despite their shorter exposure to the sun. In the sunnier areas, I grow Hydrangea paniculata 'Limelight', which produces dense cones of lime-coloured flowers in July. In midsummer the flowers transition into a creamy white colour, before turning a soft pink towards the start of autumn – this pink looks gorgeous and rich against the orange foliage of autumn trees. There is a really long season of interest, and in the winter months the flower heads maintain their shape on the plant. They look skeletal and delicate, and are adorned with a shimmering coat of frost on cold mornings. In the shadier parts of the border I grow pink mophead hydrangeas (Hydrangea macrophylla), which are better suited to semi-shade. Hydrangeas have earned their place in our garden thanks to their long season of interest, coupled with being wonderfully low-maintenance.

My absolute favourite shrub in our garden is a weigela that has been here for so many years it has grown to almost resemble a small tree. Unfortunately, we don't know the exact variety because it has been here so long, but we adore it nonetheless. The weigela is immensely popular with the pollinators in June when it is covered with hundreds of pale pink flowers, and after its first flush it tends to provide a few smaller flushes of flowers through the remainder of the summer.

We also inherited a mature lilac shrub when we moved here, and we are very grateful to whoever planted it all those years ago. In spring it is covered with huge domes of soft purple, admired by humans and pollinators alike. The flowers have a deliciously sweet scent that can be used to make sugars, syrups and sweets. I also enjoy weaving the flowering stems into a spring flower crown or wreath.

Shrub roses are another favourite in our garden. I have planted dozens of David Austin shrub roses over the years. Some of them have been given as gifts from friends and family to mark a special occasion, so the plants hold memories of particular days and particular people. Our most successful shrub roses are 'Olivia Rose Austin', for whatever reason they perform really well in our soil. Other varieties I grow include 'Silas Marner', 'Desdemona', 'Emily Brontë', 'Scepter'd Isle', 'Queen of Sweden' and 'Gentle Hermione' – all soft pink roses are welcome in my garden. Modern cultivars of rose have a good resistance to disease and will repeat flower through the summer, sometimes even into the winter. We usually get four flushes of flowers from our strongest plants, and the plants are only six years old.

Similarly to how I choose trees, I welcome shrubs that are both productive and ornamental. One such shrub is bay (*Laurus nobilis*), which grows on the edge of my herb garden and within easy reach of the kitchen so I can pop out and grab a couple of leaves to use as seasoning. Ornamentally, bay is evergreen, so it acts as a good screen between our garden and next door's garden too. I am also experimenting with growing tea (*Camellia sinensis*).

Some shrubs, like camellia, viburnum and daphne, flower and retain their foliage in winter, providing interest, structure and habitat when other plants are dormant. I have introduced some camellias to our garden, but they are slower to fill the space and are part of my long-term vision.

Consider including these flowering shrubs in your garden: rose, lavender, hydrangea, shrub roses, viburnum, lilac, weigela, mock orange, camellia, lavatera (tree mallow), flowering currant, deutzia, abelia and daphne.

Perennials

Perennials, plants living longer than two years, form the backbone of many gardens. They can be deciduous, going dormant in winter, or evergreen, maintaining some foliage year-round. Many cottage garden favourites, such as peonies, geraniums and lupins, fall into this category.

A significant advantage of many perennials is their ability to grow larger each year. After a few years, you can divide them, creating new plants to expand your garden or share with friends or neighbours. While some may take a few years to reach their full potential, their long-term growth trajectory – often described as 'sleep, creep, then leap' – makes them a rewarding investment. Perennial gardens can also be lower maintenance than annual gardens, which need re-sowing every year.

Many gardeners use a hybrid of perennials and annuals. Personally, because my energy levels can be low or fluctuating, I am building up a stock of perennial flowers that will carry me through the years when I can't give the garden as much time. Perennials are rewarding for their promise of growth and improvement over the years. Even during periods when you can't actively garden, knowing that your perennials are establishing their roots and thriving can be incredibly gratifying.

Perennials have soft, lush growth, so medium and tall plants will be susceptible to wind or rain damage without added support, and the weight of larger flowers may cause the plants to droop.

Metal **supports**, or handmade ones from flexible materials like willow, can be very effective in propping perennials upright. In my garden, I use thin metal supports to prop up peonies (see image on page 86) and oriental poppies. Some gardeners plant their perennials densely, allowing the plants to naturally support one another. It can also be helpful to use sturdy shrubs between perennials for this purpose.

Most of the perennials I grow are chosen because they bring a soft pastel colour to the garden. I grow a number of oriental poppies, my favourite being *Papaver orientale* 'Princess Victoria Louise'. The flowers are huge bowls of pastel pink, and although they don't last very long, the petals fall away to reveal a stunning green seedhead that can be dried and used in flower arrangements, or left in the garden as a focal point. I adore foxgloves, and although most are **biennials**, *Digitalis x mertonensis* is a short-lived perennial. It is a shorter, stockier foxglove, with a colour gradient of peach into crushed strawberry through its petals. I have plants that have flowered in my garden for four consecutive years, and they self-seed happily too. At the back of the border you will find spires of *Linaria* 'Peachy' and 'Dial Park' standing at a height of 1m (3ft) tall and flowering through a few weeks of summer. 'Peachy' has delicate pale yellow into peach petals, and 'Dial Park' has mauve-pink flowers. Both have an impressive stature and draw your eye to the back of the border, without being too imposing.

The front of my flower borders are planted with shorter perennials that offer good ground cover, including **hardy** geraniums (*Geranium pratense* 'Summer Skies' is a favourite of mine), *Alchemilla mollis* and *Stachys byzantina*.

Most perennials will flower in summer, and can be used to create a really impressive display at the height of the garden year. In order to extend the flowering season, it can be good to include perennials that flower later in the year, for a longer period of time, or at multiple times in one year. I try to grow lots of perennials that repeat flower, such as hardy geraniums and catmint, and I include lots of late-flowering plants like Japanese anemones, rudbeckia, echinacea and perennial sunflowers to bring life to the start of autumn. It can take a few years to build up a border that looks interesting at multiple points in the year. It's good to get into the habit of observing, reflecting and noticing gaps to fill.

A very generous perennial is *Erigeron karvinskianus* (Mexican fleabane), which produces masses of pink and white daisy-like flowers over a very long season. Mexican fleabane is popular with pollinators, can grow in poor soil, is drought tolerant and will self-seed around the garden with ease. It will happily grow in gaps in walls or steps, and places that you assume to be uninhabitable to plant life. I use it to soften hard edges and fill gaps. We have a flight of stone steps

that connect our house to our garden, and over the last five years I have been scattering the seedheads from a couple of erigeron plants to create a fully covered staircase. In summer it looks beautiful, and the plants have created an environment for insects on a previously barren space.

Perennials to consider: lupin, peony, hardy geranium, ox-eye daisy, hollyhock, dianthus, delphinium, catmint, yarrow, campanula, aquilegia, Japanese anemone, phlox, lady's mantle, rudbeckia, perennial sunflower, field scabious, coneflower, veronica, Shasta daisy and oriental poppy.

Climbing plants

Climbing plants are excellent for maximising vertical space and beautifying structures like fences or walls. Wisteria and climbing roses, for example, need support like a trellis or training wires, as they won't adhere directly to walls. Others, like Boston ivy or Virginia creeper, can attach themselves to surfaces, though it's essential to consider the potential for damage to fragile structures.

One climber I am utterly in love with is clematis, and I grow a number of them in my cottage garden. I have three types of clematis; by growing a few varieties it is possible to have flowers in the garden for three quarters of the year. The first clematis I introduced was a *Clematis montana*. The plant is completely covered in pale pink and white flowers with soft yellow centres in May, and is really useful for softening harsh walls or fences. It is one of the things I most look forward to seeing in spring. *Clematis montana* can be a vigorous climber, covering an area up to 6m (19.5ft). I also grow summer-flowering clematis varieties including 'Blue Angel', 'Piilu' and 'Miss Bateman'. These plants have larger, more vibrant colours and their overall size is smaller and better suited to pots and flower borders. I grow summer clematis up the base of trees (where there is enough light), and on hazel tripods among other perennial plants. When they flower, they are absolute showstoppers and their colourful petals really come to life in the golden hour. In the colder months, you will find winter-flowering clematis varieties such as 'Freckles' and 'Jingle Bells' flowering on our fences, adding so much beauty when the garden is largely quiet. If you want to make a strong impression with flowers in your garden, clematis is a must.

Climbing roses, while needing substantial support, offer stunning visual appeal when trained along walls or fences. Consider the aspect of the wall before planting, as different climbers thrive under varying light conditions. It's also crucial to consider the space you want to cover; some climbers, like certain rambling roses, grow vigorously and may overwhelm smaller structures but are perfect for larger ones like tall fruit trees. On our largest plum tree, I grow a white single-petal rose called 'Rambling Rector'. It is a very vigorous plant and needs a lot of space, but I love that it adds an extra flowering window within the area – in spring the tree is covered with blossom, and in summer it appears as though it is flowering again when the roses unfurl from their buds. Because it is a single-petal variety, it is easily accessible to pollinators too. Other climbing roses I grow in the garden include 'The Generous Gardener', 'Eden', 'Claire Austin' and 'James Galway'. Once they have finished flowering, they produce beautiful red rosehips, which we leave for the birds to feast on over autumn and winter.

Climbing plants can be productive too. I was pleasantly surprised to discover that we can grow kiwi vines in the UK with great success, and am in the process of establishing a vine on an archway between two of my raised beds. I also grow green and red grapes around the polytunnel. If I don't eat the fruit, the ducks eagerly snack on them.

Climbers to consider: clematis, star jasmine, honeysuckle, climbing and rambling rose, climbing hydrangea, wisteria, perennial sweet pea, passion flower, grapevine, kiwi vine and chocolate vine.

GARDEN JOBS FOR SPRING

In the fruit and vegetable garden:

- Ensure everything is set for the growing season. This includes ordering compost, finishing any mulching activities, and organising seeds if not already done. Prepare your tools and materials: gather seed trays and make plant labels to keep track of your plantings.

- Begin main seed sowing in anticipation of summer harvests. As seedlings mature, prick them out and pot them on. Once they're strong enough, start hardening off the young plants. This prepares them for outdoor conditions (see page 57).

- Plant out these young plants after the last frost in your area to avoid cold damage.

- Build supports for plants like peas and broad beans, which need structural support as they grow (see page 221).

- Regularly check for pests and take appropriate action early to prevent infestations.

- Harvest asparagus, chives, parsley and other herbs.

- Pick overwintered vegetables like kale, cabbage, leeks and year-round cauliflower. Gather food from perennial plants such as rhubarb and perennial kale.

In the flower border:

- Cut back and tidy up last year's foliage. This is crucial now as insects have finished using it over winter.

- Set up frames or stakes for plants prone to flopping over, such as peonies and oriental poppies (see page 221).

- Prune shrubs that are looking leggy, such as hydrangeas and mallows (see image overleaf).

- Spring is a great time to introduce new perennials to your flower borders (see page 77).

- **Deadhead** tulip bulbs to encourage them to focus energy back into the bulb. Feed the remaining foliage with **seaweed or comfrey fertiliser** to replenish nutrients (see pages 138 and page 171).

Lawn care:

- Encourage biodiversity. Let your grass grow to benefit pollinators and local wildlife (see page 46).

- For naturalised bulbs like snowdrops, crocuses and narcissi, leave them in unmown grass. Allow them to complete their growth cycle, ideally for four to six weeks after flowering.

Observation:

- Take time to observe the beauty of spring bulbs, forget-me-nots and the blossoming of mini meadows where they are allowed to grow.

- Appreciate the flowering of clematis and the bloom of fruit trees, and new foliage as it emerges from the soil.

Above: pruning damaged stems from a hydrangea plant. Opposite: top left, potting on a perennial kale plant grown from a cutting; top right, tying homemade plant supports with twine; bottom left, pruning leggy growth from a mallow plant; bottom right, using metal frames to support heavy peony growth.

M

S

U

M

E

R

Summer is a time of generosity.

The extended days of summer bring a sense of warmth and natural energy. At the end of June we are rewarded with the longest day of the year, and I make a point to try and absorb as much of those long evenings outside as I possibly can. Though there is plenty of plant life to tend to through the warmer months, I've learned the importance of tending to myself too, with adequate rest. I try to sit and watch as many summer sunsets as I can find the time for, and I gather fresh chamomile and lavender flowers with which to brew cups of tea. In rainier years, the showers don't stop me from getting outside in summer – I put on a waterproof coat or take shelter in the greenhouse while looking out for rainbows. The ducks very much enjoy a rainy summer's day in the garden; the moist soil invites slugs out of their damp hiding nooks and makes foraging most rewarding for the flock.

Wildlife friendly

There are plenty of creatures keeping me company in the summer garden. Newts return to the pond for their breeding season. There must be hundreds of them in our wildlife pond, and they are fascinating to watch as they dance around each other in the water. We usually spot slow worms in the garden during summer too. They are beautiful, sleek, grey legless lizards that resemble snakes in appearance. Slow worms seek habitats that are humid and shaded, feasting on small invertebrates like slugs and worms. We have noticed that our compost bins meet all of these criteria and are therefore usually home to a few. We exercise caution when loading or emptying the bins, sometimes foregoing any interference altogether if slow worms are present.

Frogs and toads can also be found in the garden through summer, and on warm evenings my partner and I enjoy watching the pipistrelle bats dart quickly around us as they catch moths, mosquitos and other insects. All of these wonderful creatures are part of a natural food chain that helps us control pests without any artificial products. Beyond

practicalities though, there is something deeply reassuring in watching wildlife in a garden. I might have had a stressful day, or spent too long staring at a computer screen, but when I sit outside and watch bats dart past within a metre of my body, or observe a newt basking in a sunny patch of water for an hour, I'm able to reconnect to the magic of life, and can put aside worry in favour of wonder as I watch the world of my garden.

Feathered friends

Our flock of ducks are energetic and at their most productive through summer. The females lay eggs most days, and the drake becomes very protective of his mates, chasing and attacking anyone who he deems to be a potential threat. I escape lightly – it's enough for him to keep a watchful eye on me while I pull weeds or water plants around him. My partner on the other hand can't catch a break, and will frequently find our drake's beak clasped around his fingers if he tries to relax in a deckchair in any part of the garden.

A backdrop of perennial cottage garden flowers keeps me feeling inspired through summer, without being too demanding in terms of upkeep. The start of the season brings the first flush of roses in various shades of pink, tall white alliums, delicate purple irises, peach-coloured foxgloves and pink oriental poppies, whose flowers are so short lived you might miss them on a windy day, but in spite of this are very much worthwhile for the beauty they bring while they are in bloom. Harsher surfaces like stone steps and walls become softened with mounds of *Erigeron karvinskianus*, which self-seeds in the most surprising of places. The abundance of flowers brings a sweet scent of pollen to the air, and a hive of pollinator activity.

Mowing the lawn

I like to mow most of the grass through summer, with the exception of the orchard which I leave for the grasshoppers to enjoy. Mowing the lawn brings a sense of orderliness to the space while the beds and borders grow wild. I use the grass clippings either in the compost bin, where they break down quickly and add nitrogen, a useful plant food, or I apply the grass clippings directly onto soil as a mulch (see page 127 for more details). I also harvest my comfrey plants three or four times through summer, adding the chopped material in hessian sacks to our water butts to create a natural plant food (see page 128 for steps on how to do this yourself). Hungry crops like tomatoes, melons and aubergines are very grateful to be fed with this liquid plant food while they produce our harvest.

As midsummer arrives, it is a time to shift my focus from growing flowers to food. From peas and garlic to broad beans, cucumbers, overwintered brassicas and the first few tomatoes, these bountiful harvests feel like a reward for nourishing the soil with nutrient-rich mulch during winter and tending to tiny seedlings through spring. During the weeks when I am low on energy, the fruit trees and perennials remain steadfast in their ability to provide us with food. Crops like loganberries, blueberries and raspberries, peaches and damsons provide a baseline harvest even when I haven't kept up with my garden routine. I am reassured by the crops that will survive and provide for several years; they give me permission to take a break if I need to.

Deterring pests

Summer isn't without challenges; in the vegetable garden there can be battles against whiteflies, cabbage white butterflies and asparagus beetles. Annoying as these creatures can be, they are part of the wider ecosystem, and I try to encourage natural predation through birds, bats, frogs and ladybirds, while also planting with natural deterrents in mind, through **companion planting** or polycultures. This involves a bit of experimentation, and the acceptance that some crops will be sacrificial. Planting plenty of different crops means you will never be entirely disappointed; some things are bound to work out. I have found that as the garden's ecosystem has built up over the years, and my planting has become more diverse, the pests may be present, but they don't tend to overwhelm plants as they would in a monocrop environment.

The strong momentum of summer sweeps past in a breeze, and the final weeks always feel like they arrive too quickly. The transition away from summer is bittersweet. The warmth and abundance of the season aren't easy to let go of, but the farewell is made easier by the last harvests of ripe tomatoes, aubergines, figs, apples and pears. I preserve our last home-grown tomatoes by making pasta sauces that will keep through autumn and winter, to carry a bit of summer's richness with us through the remainder of the year.

Welcoming ducks to the garden

Not long after we had moved into our cottage, I was getting to know my next-door neighbour through occasional chats over the fence and I asked her if she knew anything about the history of our gardens. She told me about how the gardens used to be one shared smallholding, serving the whole row of terraced cottages. She explained how her garden was previously joined with ours and was used to keep pigs. We had the skeleton of a small stone barn remaining, presumably the former pigsty; half of the barn sat in our garden and the other half of it sat next door. Our side had survived pretty well, considering it was first constructed over 250 years ago. All of the stone walls were still intact, albeit slightly crumbling on one edge where a large tree trunk had grown against the surface over time. The barn had a clay pantile roof, precariously held up by wooden beams that had become very rotten. There were no doors remaining. We had been using the barn to store firewood and garden tools, but after talking to our neighbour about the barn's previous inhabitants, it felt like a disservice to the space to use it for storing clutter. We made a promise to ourselves that we would bring life back to the space and keep a flock of ducks in there.

Since it took a while for us to repair the barn and to get the garden ready for keeping ducks, I had some time to research different duck varieties and to get some outside opinions on which breed to choose. One of the things I had to keep in mind was that we didn't have a large pond, and the pond that we did have I wanted to keep duck-free in the interest of protecting the newts that already made the water their home. A number of people (including my grandad) recommended runner ducks, a breed that are happy foraging in the garden as long as they have access to a deep bucket or small paddling pool of water. Runner ducks are very entertaining to watch. They have a very long, thin neck and stand in an upright posture; because of this they are sometimes described by their owners as 'bowling pin ducks', 'wine bottles', or 'garden penguins', among other amusing nicknames.

Thanks to the imagery of Beatrix Potter, I had imagined keeping a group of plump white Aylesbury ducks that would stroll graciously past

foxgloves wearing tiny blue bonnets. Runner ducks didn't really fit this idyllic image. They are awkward, colourful, goofy creatures that dart off in a sprint at unpredictable intervals. But we warmed to them so quickly, and apart from their use in the garden they make wonderful pets. We currently have three apricot runner ducks, named Waylon, Abigail and Coco, who we welcomed to the garden on a sunny summer's day.

Eggs

Runner ducks are particularly good layers compared to other duck breeds, with females laying 200–300 eggs per year on average. Egg production is seasonal, and the ducks will stop laying when they moult their feathers in autumn. Like many things in the garden, ducks remind us to slow down and rest through the colder months before we regain momentum in spring. Our flock usually resume daily laying at the start of March, as the temperatures warm up and daylight hours increase. As the ducks age, they won't lay as heavily, but for the first four or five years of their life they give plenty of eggs. I am convinced the eggs taste even better after the ducks have had more time free-ranging and foraging for their own food (instead of only eating poultry pellets in their pen).

Runner ducks don't tend to go broody, so they are unlikely to hatch their own eggs. Our females have very little interest in becoming parents, and have been known to drop their eggs in random locations while foraging in the garden. The most we have come to expect from them is a nest in the corner of their enclosure. The girls will take it in turns to lay into the nest, and then abandon it completely until the next morning when it's time to lay again. Other breeds of ducks may be more likely to sit on a nest and incubate their eggs, so this can be something to consider when deciding on a breed.

Compared to chicken eggs, duck eggs are slightly larger, with a much richer yolk. They are a good source of omega-3, and are excellent for baking cakes with. One of the first pieces of advice I was given from other duck owners was to bake a cake with the eggs, and now I won't bake a cake without them. I don't know exactly why, but duck eggs bind ingredients together exceptionally well and help create a perfect consistency in baked goods.

It always feels like a treat when I head out to feed the ducks in the morning and there is a nest of eggs in the corner of their pen, the shells a beautiful mix of soft blue hues. Our mornings in spring and summer, when the ducks are at their most productive, are filled with cooked full English breakfasts or scrambled eggs on toast. It is one of many comforting, seasonal rhythms that the garden gives us.

A natural pest control

Ducks are great foragers, and love nothing more than snacking on a juicy slug found in the vegetable patch. Unlike chickens, ducks don't scratch the soil while exploring the garden, so they can be slightly less destructive in that regard. They can flatten tender plants while looking for things to eat, so I am always careful to keep them off my tulip patch in spring, and away from tender perennials throughout summer.

Ducks will forage for slugs, snails, beetles, larvae, grasshoppers and plenty of other small creatures. They have helped us immensely with slug control in the garden. Before we had ducks, there were some plants that I just could not grow because the slug population would eat every fragment of foliage, such as lupins and cabbages.

The only place the ducks don't offer pest control is the greenhouse, because the seedling tables are too high up for them to reach. I try to maintain a habit of picking slugs off our seed trays and collecting them in a bucket, and giving this to the ducks as a treat.

The downside of ducks being such excellent foragers is that they can be prone to eating some of the wildlife we try to keep in our gardens, such as toads, frogs and newts. We are really lucky to share our garden with such a thriving community of newts. We try to keep the newts safe by dividing the garden into different zones. The ducks are mostly kept near my flower borders and vegetable plants, where we will benefit the most from them eating slugs and insects. We keep them away from the wildlife pond, especially when the newts are breeding there in spring.

Duck compost

I have learned that taking good care of the soil is a necessity. Healthy soil is the foundation for healthy plants. We try to disturb it as little as possible, keeping the surface covered with a layer of mulch or plant life, and by replenishing the nutrients that our crops take out of the soil through their growth cycle. Before we had ducks, I used to buy a huge delivery of compost every autumn, and add this as a top layer to my growing space. In principle it worked well, but in practice it was a huge amount of effort, most notably because our garden is landscaped into the edge of a steep valley and there is no road access. Lugging a tonne of compost up a 91m (300ft) slope, two plastic buckets at a time, got old pretty quickly. Now that we have the ducks, I use their waste to nourish the soil instead.

Duck waste is high in **nitrogen, phosphorus and potassium** – the three components of the fertilisers you can buy in the garden centre. It is more nutrient-dense than chicken waste and, unlike other types of manure, you can add it to the soil right away without it burning your plants. When I clean our ducks' barn out, I spread the manure directly onto the soil as a mulch for my roses and a filling for our raised beds.

With edible crops, I add the manure to my compost heap for at least half a year before adding to the surface of the soil, to avoid any risk from pathogens around our food harvests.

The joy of companionship

Even if ducks didn't bring so much value to the garden, I would still want them for the sheer joy of keeping them. Ducks are often described by gardeners as a thing of utility, and their usefulness can't be denied, but for us they are first and foremost cherished pets. On the days when I am overstimulated and struggling, I make it my main mission to sit outside with a cup of herbal tea and watch the ducks as they free-range, even if I can only face doing so for a quarter of an hour. They never fail to comfort me. The girls are quite chatty, and if you sit yourself in the garden they will run up to you in excitement. When I am at my most overwhelmed, I can lose the ability to speak, which feels like quite a lonely experience in a world that prioritises outward expression. Being around animals that don't require you to speak, and who welcome your company irrespective of your mood, is a delightfully comforting thing.

DUCK TIPS

It's important to consider both the positives and the challenges that can come with owning any pet. As fabulous as ducks are for the garden, there are some points to weigh up before buying or hatching them.

Choosing your flock

Ducks are social creatures and should be kept in at least a pair so that they always have company. Male ducks can be aggressive, especially in spring and summer when it is mating season. Our drake is fine from a distance, but he will try to pinch you if he catches you. As far as he is concerned, all creatures beyond himself are a threat to his reproductive success. Thanks to the aggressive protection and mating behaviours of male ducks, mating season is usually referred to as 'silly season' by duck owners. As soon as autumn arrives, our drake undergoes a complete personality metamorphosis, becoming tame and cuddly, and likes to be around humans again.

You may decide it is easier to keep a flock of female ducks, without having any drakes at all. Including a drake within the flock supposedly increases egg production and provides protection from predators. It is generally advised that ducks are kept in a ratio of 3:1 females to males, to prevent male infighting, and to ensure the females aren't over mated by males. Male ducks can also be content in a 'bachelor' flock, and will happily cohabit with one another providing there aren't any females to fight over.

Keep in mind that the gender ratio of your flock is beyond your control if you are hatching ducklings yourself from a batch of fertile eggs. You may well end up with a flock of mostly drakes that are sweet and endearing as ducklings, but within two seasons have decided to try and rip each other to shreds. It is advisable to not hatch your own flock and instead rescue an existing flock of adults or buy a flock from a local farm. It is surprisingly easy to rescue ducks through groups on social media.

Preparing for mud and mess

If I could only warn prospective duck owners about one thing, it would be the mess. Unless you have a huge plot of land, the area where you house your ducks will almost certainly become something reminiscent of a bog. The ducks themselves don't mind this, as long as they have a clean and dry place to sleep and access to fresh water so they can keep clean. But to a gardener who is precious about their space, the mess can be quite a shock. We have a fenced-off area where the ducks live for most of the time, and when we are gardening or spending time outdoors we invite the ducks to free-range with us. The fenced-off area started life as a lawn, and within a month or so it had transitioned into ... mud. We change the bedding regularly, so their indoor barn area is always clean, especially through the winter when the mud is particularly wet. Cleaning the barn out can be quite a lot of work, as it involves transporting multiple wheelbarrows of soiled straw to the compost bin at the top of the garden. The mess is heavier than you would expect.

Potential predators

Our garden borders on a field that is semi-wild and therefore home to plenty of wildlife. We have foxes, badgers and birds of prey that regularly visit the garden. For the first two years of keeping ducks, we used to let them free-range the garden between sunrise and sunset. A nearby fox became wise to our routine, and struck one of our ducks to feed its cubs at the start of spring. We had expected our dogs to protect the ducks, but they sat on the ground and watched the entire scenario without flinching. Thankfully my partner noticed what had happened and chased the fox away before it could take any of the other ducks, but the fox returned to the garden daily for weeks after its successful catch. We also reinforced the mesh on their enclosure, and added a layer of mesh on the ground around the edge of the pen, where foxes are likely to tunnel their way in. Mink, stoat and weasels will also prey on young ducks. If you live outside of the UK the list of potential predators may be entirely different, so it is important to research and prepare in order to keep your flock safe.

Uninvited guests

Keeping poultry in your garden will invariably attract other creatures who are interested in eating your flock's food. This might be rats or mice, and if your enclosure isn't covered you may also attract rooks and magpies. Rats multiply very quickly, and we had a real problem with them in the early days of keeping ducks. One of the best prevention strategies is to get a vermin-proof treadle feeder, and train your ducks to use this. We tried three different models, and the only one that was truly vermin-proof was a large one called 'Grandpa's Feeder'. The ducks stand on a step to raise the lid on the feeder. Rats are perfectly capable of understanding how this works, but they aren't heavy enough to open the feeder themselves. Your ducks will learn to use the feeder much faster than you expect, and as soon as one of them gets the hang of it the others should follow. It took our ducks about five days to confidently use the feeder, after which the rat population declined quickly without access to food.

Bumblefoot and flu

Ducks are generally healthy creatures, but as with all pets you should be prepared to monitor their health and take them to the vet when necessary. Problems you may encounter include bumblefoot, ducks becoming eggbound, eye infections, prolapses, wet feather and avian flu. Ducks can be clumsy and may trip over things – we have encountered a few sprained legs over the years for this reason.

A long-term commitment

Pet ducks live on average for 10–15 years, with some even living into their 20s. This should be considered when you are thinking of starting a flock.

WHAT DO DUCKS NEED?
A PRACTICAL OVERVIEW FOR ASPIRING DUCK KEEPERS

Keeping ducks in your garden can be a rewarding experience. To ensure your ducks lead healthy, happy lives, there are several key needs to consider:

Company
Ducks are social creatures that thrive in the company of their own kind. It's recommended to keep at least two ducks to prevent loneliness.

Nutrition
A balanced diet is crucial for ducks. They require a diet rich in niacin, which can be provided through specialised duck pellets. Supplementing their diet with vegetables and fruits can add variety and extra nutrition.

Ducks need calcium for strong eggshells and overall health. Providing crushed eggshells or seashells as part of their diet is an effective way to supplement their calcium intake. Ensure these are crushed finely enough to prevent any risk of choking.

Regular worming, either as required or every six months, is important to keep ducks healthy and free from parasites.

Water
Ducks need clean, fresh water available at all times, deep enough to submerge their heads for drinking and cleaning their nostrils. While runner ducks may not require a pond, other breeds may require access to a larger water body for swimming. This not only meets their physical needs but also provides significant mental and emotional enrichment.

Housing
A predator-proof shelter is essential to protect ducks from potential threats like foxes, badgers and birds of prey. The housing should offer:

- Weather protection against rain, wind and extreme temperatures.

- Enough space for all ducks to rest comfortably, with a minimum of 0.5m^2 (1.6ft^2) per duck for sleeping areas.

- Clean bedding, such as straw, to maintain hygiene and comfort.

Space to roam
Ducks benefit greatly from having enough space to roam and forage. A minimum of 1.5m^2 (5ft^2) per duck in a secure pen is advisable, though more space is ideal to promote well-being. Safe free-ranging areas allow ducks to exhibit natural behaviours such as foraging, which is crucial for their mental stimulation and overall happiness.

Generous plants and perennials for your edible garden

Perennial plants, those that have a lifecycle longer than two years, are generous entities that can really minimise effort on the gardener's part. So much of traditional vegetable growing revolves around annual crops. The sowing window begins with a big effort at the start of spring: we devote many hours to raising plants from seed, we gradually harden them off, plant them into bare soil, and after we have got what we wanted from them, we rip the plants out and replenish the lost nutrients back into the soil, ahead of repeating the pattern again the following year. It's a tried-and-tested pattern that works, but if we add perennial edible plants into our rhythm, we can make things both easier for ourselves and we can be kinder to our soil.

Soil health   Soil is composed of living organisms, and in order to keep our soil healthy, we should look to preserve as much of this life as we can. When we grow annual vegetables alone, their roots exist in the soil for less than a year before they die or we remove and replace them. This regular uprooting can disrupt the beneficial fungal web within our soil, and degrade the structure of our soil, making it more prone to erosion and drying out. When we add perennials into the planting mix, they set down a more permanent root system that helps to maintain soil structure and health while annuals come and go around them. These longstanding root systems keep soil porous and light, and therefore assist in better water retention for all plants in the local network. Long-lasting root systems also preserve the mycorrhizal fungi network, which helps plants to distribute nutrients and share pest and disease warnings between themselves. Perennial plants also capture carbon from the atmosphere, making them a valuable tool in our resistance to climate change. You add them to the garden once, and they will help maintain it for you for years to come.

Growing perennial plants alleviates effort for the gardener when compared to growing annuals, in that we plant them once and reap the rewards of harvests for many years to come. Perennials can also be used

to grow food through times of the year when annual harvests are scarcer, extending the window of productivity in our gardens. For me, it isn't a matter of preferring annuals or perennials over the other. I love growing annuals like French beans and tomatoes too much to ever garden without them, but I can also see how adding some chamomile or perennial kale in the space around these crops is good for the soil in the long term.

One of the most appealing things about perennial crops for me is that often they are somewhat unusual. This fills me with excitement, and makes me want to share them with everyone I know. When I first discovered that perennial onions exist, and that you don't have to grow them from seed every year, I shared so much of my crop with my friends that I barely had anything left to actually eat. Though my garden-to-plate journey there was unyielding, that sharing of substance, joy and knowledge between loved ones is a core part of what food growing is about.

Perennial plants are amazingly resilient to pests and adverse weather conditions. There have been summers when whitefly and cabbage white caterpillars have been particularly difficult to control in the garden. My annual broccoli doesn't stand a chance without the protection of a fine mesh, but my perennial kale plants can be completely stripped to the stems and they will still return with great vigour once the flies have been eaten by a predator or killed by cold temperatures. Their deep root system also makes them resilient against drought, as they rely less on the soil surface that dries most easily, and are able to draw moisture from deep within the ground.

Modern cultivars of annual vegetables have been bred to be large, glossy and showy. Perennial vegetables that have been passed between gardeners via cuttings and tubers aren't always as visually impressive. Sometimes perennial crops are a bit smaller, less uniform, or they may be tougher to harvest or prepare. But the benefits of low maintenance and ongoing soil care are too valuable to ignore.

Edible perennials

Many growers will be familiar with some edible perennials already. Most allotments house a well-established rhubarb plant, a collection of strawberries, and perhaps a patch of horseradish that has run wild over the years. But there is a whole world beyond those familiar favourites. After gardening for a few years and falling in love with perennial plants, I have come to view my edible garden in layers. The bones of the garden are the fruit trees – apples, pears, cherries, nectarines and figs. Then there is a layer of long-living shrubs and woody plants, things like gooseberries, tayberries, raspberries, my kiwi vine and goji berry bushes. Next is a layer of edible perennials including onions, kale, asparagus and rhubarb. The remaining space is embellished with whatever annuals I choose to grow in that year, most likely tomatoes, courgettes and beans. All of these plants are dotted among each other, and their diversity creates a thriving community and a bountiful harvest.

Sourcing edible perennial plants can be difficult. Seed catalogues lean towards the fashion of growing large, uniform crops, and it's in their best interest for us to be purchasing annual seeds every year. I have built up our perennial food collection from swaps with local allotment owners, ordering cuttings and seeds from perennial nurseries, and joining specialist groups on social media. Building the collection is an ongoing process. There are still many more perennial vegetables I would like to grow, but I have not yet been able to source them. It may not make economic sense for large garden centres to stock perennial vegetables, but when you meet someone who is enthusiastic about growing them, they will often want to share their enthusiasm with as many gardeners as possible, so I remain hopeful that our collection of plants will continue to expand in the years ahead.

PERENNIAL PLANTS IN MY EDIBLE GARDEN

In the raised beds behind my polytunnel, you will find my beloved collection of perennial plants. Many of these plants have been here for several years, and they happily take care of themselves while I work on gardening the areas around them. The perennials are so tolerant of whatever weather or pests the garden throws at them, and yet so generous when it comes to harvesting.

Asparagus (early and late)

Growing asparagus requires a bit of delayed gratification but will bring generous rewards after you've given it some patience. After planting asparagus crowns in the garden, it's best to leave them for two or three years before harvesting, so they have time to establish a strong root system. After this, you can pick the spears every couple of days throughout springtime, and the plants can live for as long as 25 years. I grow two varieties in my garden to extend the harvest period – 'Gijnlim' can be cut from mid-spring, and 'Guelph Millennium' is ready in late spring/early summer. I was in such a hurry to get them established, they were the first thing I planted in my vegetable garden four years ago.

Perennial kale (Daubenton's)

I was given a cutting of Daubenton's perennial kale a few years ago, and it has become one of my prized possessions in the vegetable garden. I leave it well alone in the corner of the garden, where it happily withstands all pest and weather damage, growing larger every year. The plant grows in compact mounds and roots very easily from cuttings, so as soon as you have one mature plant, you can create a great deal more from it. Daubenton's kale has a beautiful light green colouring, and if you are lucky, you may find a cutting with a **variegated** leaf. The leaves can be harvested at any point in the year and cooked in place of kale or other greens; they have a mild and nutty flavour.

Purple tree collard

I was sent a purple tree collard cutting from a fellow gardener and grew it entirely out of fascination for its height and colour. Tree collards can grow beyond 2m (6.6ft) tall. Ours grew almost as tall as me before we sadly lost it to a very cold winter, though this is unusual as tree collards are hardy once established. They are strange and beautiful-looking plants. The leaves have a striking gradient of colour, with vibrant green centres and purple stems and perimeters, appearing almost otherworldly. The young leaves are best blanched as a side dish or used in stir-fries. Larger leaves can be tougher in texture, but they make fantastic kale chips when roasted with a little oil.

Walking onions

Walking onions (*Allium × proliferum*) are exceptionally useful and productive plants to include in your vegetable garden. There are three main parts to the plant – a central bulb, a stem and bulbils that grow on top of the stem where you might expect a flower. As the bulbils grow too heavy to be held up by the stem, they collapse onto a patch of nearby soil and sprout new onions, hence the name 'walking onions'. All parts of the plant are edible, though the bulbils are so small they aren't worth the preparation time. The central bulb is similar to a red onion, albeit smaller and so a little fiddlier to prepare. It has a beautifully strong taste and can be used in place of onion in cooking. When young and soft, the stems can be used in place of spring onions. The plants are perennial until you eat the main bulb, so we grow enough of them that we can harvest the main bulbs and stems from some plants, while leaving neighbouring onions to produce bulbils and maintain the collection.

Everlasting onions

Everlasting onions (*Allium cepa* 'Perutile') are perennial onions that don't flower, instead multiplying via division of the main bulb. When left in the garden to spread, they form clumps that can be harvested or lifted and divided to produce more clumps. In the kitchen, the green shoots can be used as you would use a spring onion, and the bulbs can be used in place of regular onions. The bulbs are small, about the size of a small shallot, so they are slightly more effort to peel and prepare, but they make up for this by being one of the lowest maintenance crops in the vegetable garden.

Perennial leeks (poireau perpétuel)

Everlasting leeks are a practical treasure for the vegetable garden. They're cut just above the ground each spring, effortlessly regrowing from their bulbs below through winter. While slightly slimmer, they're almost as big as leeks grown from seed and carry a unique flavour that's like a combination of leeks with a hint of garlic. If allowed, they'll bloom with a crown of bulbils, which you can plant to increase your supply or share with friends. They're straightforward to grow and look after, making them an ideal choice for both novice and experienced gardeners.

Rhubarb

Rhubarb is a perennial classic in the garden, known for its early harvests. It can be forced for an even earlier yield, involving a simple process of covering the plants to encourage faster, more tender growth. It's important to remove any flowering shoots, which helps the plant focus its energy on follicle production. Rhubard tastes tart, perfect for a variety of desserts, especially crumbles and puddings.

Jerusalem artichoke (or sunchokes)

Jerusalem artichokes are known for their edible tubers, which multiply underground. They can be harvested and eaten, with a few left in the soil to ensure next year's crop. By the end of summer, the tubers produce small yellow flowers similar to sunflowers, which add a layer of beauty to the vegetable garden. There are a few varieties to choose from. We were given a bag of tubers from a friend who had run out of space for them in her allotment, so ours are of an unknown variety. Jerusalem artichokes can be invasive and are best kept in a pot or raised bed to prevent undue spreading. In the kitchen they are a versatile ingredient, and can be pureed, stewed or roasted. They're particularly fibrous and can cause digestive discomfort for some, so it's best to prepare them with a bit of lemon juice to aid digestion and taste test a small amount before serving them as the heart of a dish.

Globe artichoke

Globe artichokes are statement plants in any garden, requiring a significant amount of space – up to 90cm (3ft) wide and 1.5m (5ft) tall – for a relatively small yield. However, they double as ornamental plants, fitting well into flower borders with their striking appearance. The key to harvesting artichokes is timing; pick the flower buds while still tightly closed before they bloom in summer. If left to flower, they produce stunning purple blooms that attract bees and other pollinators, adding beauty and biodiversity to your garden. I grow them purely for the appreciation of the plant, rather than using them in the kitchen.

Strawberries

Strawberries are one of the easiest fruits to grow, with shallow roots that make them perfect for ground cover around deeper-rooted plants like asparagus. They are a fantastic plant for beginner gardeners. Home-grown strawberries offer generous yields, boasting a sweetness and flavour that supermarket varieties rarely match. As summer ends, each plant produces runners, promising new plants that can be potted or planted directly into the ground. Homegrown strawberries can be popular with mice and other wildlife, so a protective cage might be necessary to safeguard your crop.

Chives

Chives, one of the smaller members of the allium family, bloom with beautiful purple flowers by late spring. They are a cut-and-come-again crop; harvesting the green shoots encourages new growth from the bulbs below. Allowing the flowers to develop can attract pollinators, enhancing the biodiversity of your garden. I grow chives along the edge of my vegetable beds and borders, which adds a layer of beauty while they are in flower, and invites pollinators towards my other crops. Dividing the clumps every few years can help spread their joy even further around the garden. Known for their pest-repelling scent, chives can also protect neighbouring plants, such as carrots, from pests like carrot fly.

Roman chamomile

Roman chamomile is a creeping, shallow-rooted perennial that serves both aesthetic and practical purposes. Its flowers can be harvested and dried for calming teas, while also attracting pollinators when left to grow. The dense mats formed by chamomile plants suppress weeds and help maintain soil moisture, making them an excellent ground cover. These plants are easily divided and transplanted to spread their serene beauty and utility throughout the garden. I grow patches of chamomile throughout the length of my polytunnel, and the scent that fills the air after watering is something I look forward to every year.

Mint

Mint is incredibly easy to grow and offers a refreshing flavour for teas and culinary dishes. To prevent it from becoming invasive, it's best grown in pots or contained spaces. Mint flowers in summer, attracting a variety of bees, butterflies, moths and other pollinators with its blooms. Its scent is also known to repel certain pests, including aphids, ants and mosquitoes, making it a valuable addition to any garden for both its utility and appeal.

Growing with nature

The summer garden is brimming with wildlife that also call our gardens home. A number of wild species can actually assist us in gardening, too. Pollinators help with fruit production as they pollinate the flowers on our edible plants. Hedgehogs, foxes, slow worms and frogs can assist in our slug removal efforts, and parasitic wasps can help keep caterpillar populations under control while we eagerly watch our brassicas grow.

I like to consider ways I can support plant and soil life in my garden through summer, helping them remain resilient through periods of harsh heat and drought.

Using natural mulches

To mulch the soil means to add a thin layer of natural material to its surface, with the aim of preserving soil health. Mulches protect the soil from erosion, preserve moisture and regulate the temperature of the soil. Mulches also suppress weed germination, because they smother any unwanted seeds with a layer of material thick enough to deprive the seeds from light. The final benefit of mulches is that they return nutrients to the soil as the organic matter breaks down. In summer, when temperatures are hot, rainfall may be scarce and weeds are quickly germinating, mulches bring us a number of useful benefits.

I tend to empty my compost bins in winter, and this is when I apply my main mulch to the garden. However, by summertime, some of this needs topping up, particularly in areas where I grow more annual vegetables and therefore disturb the soil more. In summer I use grass clippings as a mulch, because they are very easy to come by, and mulching with them saves me carrying the clippings all the way to the top of the hill where our compost bins live. I will add a layer of grass clippings about 2.5cm (1in) thick around the base of new plants, onto the surface of vegetable beds, and on the soil in my polytunnel to help conserve water and cool the soil during hot spells. If it's going to rain, I will thin the grass layer by half, to prevent it going sludgy.

Grass isn't the most aesthetically pleasing of mulches; it can go from green to yellow to beige, and it looks uneven in texture and a bit sloppy as it decays. But I constantly try to challenge my expectations of tidiness in the garden. If something brings an ecological benefit at the cost of looking messy, I try to spend some time with my discomfort and ask myself, *why do I need this area to look tidy? Isn't it more important that the area is healthy?* Though the mulch itself may look unusual, the minute the tomato plants above it produce glossy red fruits, my attention is directed there instead. The unsightly mulch is one of the main reasons my tomatoes are able to flourish and look so beautiful.

You can experiment with different mulch materials and see what works best in your growing space – some gardeners may find that grass clippings act as a slug habitat or go sludgy. Alternatives include compost, straw, sheep's wool, woodchips or even seashells (shells won't return nutrients to your soil, but will look pretty, last a long time and regulate moisture and temperature). If you decide that it is important for your garden to look tidy, then a compost mulch will do an excellent job.

Storing rainwater

Mulching our soil means that our plants don't need watering as often, because the soil is better at retaining moisture. However, it is inevitable that in the warmth of summer newly planted perennials or annual vegetable plants will need a bit of watering. Rainwater is great for this purpose because it is free, readily available and has a lower pH than tap water. In our garden we have guttering installed along the edge of our greenhouse and shed roofing, which we use to fill up two large water butts made from reclaimed whiskey barrels. When it rains, the barrels fill up, and then we use this stored rainwater to water our plants through dry periods. When full, these two reclaimed barrels allow us to water the polytunnel for a couple of weeks between showers.

Homemade plant feed

Many perennial and permanent plants may not need as much fertiliser as gardeners tend to expect; as long as we are keeping our soil healthy this should be enough to sustain them. However, annual vegetables such as tomatoes or melons can be hungry through summer, while they spend a lot of energy putting on new growth and providing us with fruit. For these plants I like to make a homemade comfrey and nettle liquid feed. Nettles are high in nitrogen, which promotes new leafy growth, and comfrey is high in potassium, which promotes flower production and fruiting. Note that if you are introducing comfrey plants to your garden, it can spread and potentially dominate a space. You may want to contain it within a bed or look for a variety than doesn't take over. Comfrey fertiliser also has a very strong smell when used to make liquid feed, so don't worry when this happens – it means you have done a good job.

To make a concentrated liquid feed, I fill a bucket with chopped comfrey and nettle leaves. The ratio is based wholly on what is available in the garden – usually slightly more comfrey leaves than nettle, but it is not a precise science for me. I crush in as many leaves as I possibly can, and sit a brick on top to compress them. Then I fill the bucket with water, and put it in a shaded and cool spot in the shed for a couple of weeks to infuse. After a fortnight or so, I strain the liquid into a large bottle and empty the leaf remnants directly onto the soil or compost where they can finish breaking down. This concentrated liquid feed can be added to a watering can at nine parts water, one part feed. I use it once every week or two on my annual fruit and vegetable plants.

I also create comfrey and nettle infusions in our water butts. For this I fill a hessian bag or cotton pillowcase with chopped leaves, and let it infuse in the water for a month or so. Once I have finished with it, I put

the whole bag on the compost heap where it will break down. This method involves a lot more water compared to making the concentrated feed, so the solution doesn't need to be watered down once it's made.

Habitat conservation

Conserving habitats within our gardens supports wildlife and encourages natural predation, which in turn benefits our plants by maintaining a balanced ecosystem. At the heart of this is embracing a little more mess.

I try to reference the natural world when planning and maintaining our garden, and emulate some of the beneficial processes found in woodland sites where fallen trees and decaying wood often remain in situ, forming natural habitats for an array of insects. In summer when I am **pruning** trees, I try to create a few 'dead hedges' or stacked logs around the edge of the garden, these offer a place to live for wildlife big and small. We can also add more intentional wildlife structures to our gardens, including ponds and bird baths, which provide birds with somewhere to wash and drink from while water is scarce.

If mining bees have made a home in the lawn, as they do every summer in our garden, or if bats have taken to roost in the shed, we consider if they are causing harm, and if not, we let them be. More often than not, these creatures can coexist with us, and are actually a helpful part of the garden ecosystem.

If, for any reason, wildlife needs to be relocated, please seek out a specialist who can move the animals safely, rather than resorting to destruction. Every garden, regardless of its size, has the potential to become a haven for wildlife. By making small, conscious changes, we can have a big impact on the natural world.

Companion planting

Companion planting is a form of polyculture that is deeply rooted in indigenous wisdom, offering numerous benefits that enhance garden productivity and ecological harmony. This method maximises space utilisation, facilitates beneficial nutrient exchanges, aids in pest control and encourages pollinator visitation, all while fostering a symbiotic relationship between different plant species.

A classic example of companion planting is the three-sisters method, traditionally employed by the Iroquois (Haudenosaunee) among other indigenous peoples of North America. This technique involves planting sweetcorn, beans and squash together. The corn provides a natural trellis for the beans to climb, while the beans fix nitrogen in the soil, benefiting all three plants. The squash spreads along the ground, acting as a living mulch that conserves moisture and suppresses weeds, creating a microenvironment where these plants can thrive together.

Plants with stronger scents can be useful companion plants in their ability to confuse or deter pests. I like to plant basil, for example, alongside tomatoes or asparagus, because it repels whiteflies and asparagus beetles with its aromatic scent.

Flowering plants like nasturtiums and calendula attract pollinators into our growing spaces, which can help pollinate our edible crops and allow for fruit to grow. In recent years I have started growing all kinds of flowers around my fruit and vegetable plants, some edible and others ornamental. I let forget-me-nots self-seed freely, and I introduce perennials with a long flowering season such as rudbeckia. Though I started doing this for the pollinators, it has evolved to include beauty that I find satisfying, too. I grow things like roses and clematis around the edge of my perennial kale, simply because I love the flowers.

Flowering edibles

When you notice that your edible crops are starting to flower, leave some of them in situ to live out their full life cycle. These flowers serve as an open invitation to beneficial predators, including parasitic wasps. The larvae of these wasps are natural allies in your garden, voraciously consuming those troublesome caterpillars and aphids that threaten your kale and other harvests. From these flowering crops you will also be able to save your own seeds.

Seeds collected from your garden will be perfectly adapted to your local growing conditions, so they stand a good chance of survival compared to what you would buy in the supermarket or garden centre.

When the time comes to clear your edible crops, snip them at the soil surface instead of pulling them out entirely. By leaving the roots in place, you contribute to the preservation of soil structure and initiate a natural process where the roots decompose, gradually releasing nutrients back into the earth. This method minimises disturbance to the soil's composition and enhances its fertility for future planting, ensuring your garden remains a nourishing and productive environment.

WHAT AM I SOWING IN SUMMER?

Though summer is a time primarily for harvesting, it is also a time to keep up the momentum in our seed-sowing efforts.

Peas are often thought of as a spring crop, but they can be sown throughout early and mid-summer to bring an extended harvest. Peas are also wonderful for maintaining soil health and nutrition because they transform atmospheric nitrogen into nitrogen in the soil around their roots, in turn feeding other plants. This process, known as nitrogen fixation, is crucial for natural soil enrichment. When you have finished with your pea plants, leave the roots in place to break down naturally in the soil.

One of my favourite foods, French beans, can be sown at the start of summer. They will put on growth extremely quickly and be cropping within a few weeks. I sow a few rounds of dwarf French beans through June and July to ensure a constant supply for the kitchen. Climbing beans crop for a longer period, so they only need to be sown once at the start of summer next to a hazel rod frame or bamboo tripod, and then they can be harvested through the remainder of the season.

Some summer sowings and plantings, including swede, cauliflower and potatoes, take longer to mature and are therefore sown or planted with autumn and winter harvests in mind. Swede, for example, requires a longer growing season and is typically ready for harvest in late autumn or winter.

Cauliflower, depending on the variety, can be sown in summer for a winter harvest, benefiting from the cooler temperatures.

Potatoes planted in late summer can be harvested as 'new' potatoes in autumn, offering a fresh, tender option late in the season. Purple sprouting broccoli is sown in summer to be harvested the following spring, providing a nutritious and vibrant addition to early-year meals.

I try to sow certain flower seeds through summer to mimic the patterns we see in nature. At the start of summer, we see seedheads develop on forget-me-nots as they ready themselves to self-seed around the garden. If we wish to sow any from seed packets, we can emulate this timeframe in our seed trays. The same is true of foxgloves – after they have flowered in early summer, they will develop a spire of seedheads that will fall to the ground. To help disperse these, I pick the dried seedheads and shake them onto bare patches of soil where they will hopefully germinate and flower the following year. Sometimes I am interested in introducing new varieties to the garden, such as the soft yellow *Digitalis purpurea* 'Lemoncello', or the delicate pink variety 'Dalmatian Peach'. Again, I take cues from natural rhythms, sowing these when the wild foxgloves drop their seed in early to mid-summer.

MONTH	FOOD	FLOWERS
● June	· Basil · Beetroot · Carrots · Cauliflower · Climbing beans · Coriander · Dill · French beans · Parsley · Peas · Potatoes · Purple sprouting broccoli · Radish · Spring onions · Swede	· Calendula · Echinacea · Forget-me-nots · Foxgloves · Lupins · Nasturtiums · Sunflowers
● July	· Beetroot · Chard · Coriander · Dill · Japanese greens · Kohlrabi · Lettuce · Parsley · Radish · Spinach · Spring onions · Turnips	· Delphiniums · Foxgloves · Marigolds
● August	· Dill · Japanese greens · Lettuce · Radish · Spinach · Spring onions	· Aquilegia · Calendula · Winter pansies

GARDEN JOBS FOR SUMMER

In the fruit and vegetable garden:

- Harvest your summer crops. At the start of the season, we enjoy harvests of broad beans, garlic and peas, followed by strawberries, summer-fruiting raspberries, blueberries, damsons, cucumbers, aubergines, onions, French beans, courgettes and tomatoes. We finish the season with sweetcorn, autumn-fruiting raspberries, climbing beans, squashes and pumpkins.

- Sow vegetable seeds throughout the summer (see page 137) to extend the growing season through autumn and winter.

- Pinch out side-shoots on tomato plants (see image overleaf).

- Water and feed your crops as required (see page 128).

- Make homemade nettle and comfrey fertiliser to feed your crops (see overleaf and page 134).

- In hot periods, add a layer of mulch around the base of your crops to help maintain moisture (see page 127). This can be compost, grass clippings, straw, sheep's wool or other organic material.

In the flower border:

- Clip mature hedges to maintain their shape. I use a battery-powered cordless trimmer for this, as it is much faster than trimming with hand tools. Ensure there are no nesting birds in the hedges before trimming (see page 70).

- Deadhead repeat-flowering roses to encourage further flushes of flowers.

- Weed around plants as required. To preserve soil nutrients, add the chopped weeds to the soil surface or a compost bin where they will break down.

- Water new plants during dry periods, as their root systems aren't deep enough to tolerate drought yet.

- Prune trees to reduce their overall size (winter pruning generally encourages new growth, while summer pruning inhibits it).

- Notice if there are any gaps in the flower border throughout the season, and take note of plants that could be used to fill these.

General garden care:

- Mow the lawn regularly in areas you wish to keep tidy, and let it grow naturally in wilder areas. Consider mowing central paths through wild areas (see page 93).

- Add grass clippings, chopped weeds and other green waste to the compost bin. Top this up with brown waste such as brown cardboard or waste paper to create a well-balanced compost.

- Consider installing a rainwater harvesting system to collect water for irrigation (see page 128).

- Check for pests and diseases regularly and take organic control measures if necessary (see page 94).

Observation:

- Make the most of the warm weather and the long evenings. For all the hours you spend working in the garden through summer, remember to incorporate rest into your routine too.

- Notice the beauty in summer flowers and wildlife. Pull up a chair and observe bees and butterflies on your flowers, or watch the pond as newts and frogs swim between plants.

Above: pinching out side shoots on a tomato plant. Opposite: top left, harvesting broad beans; top right, shaping ligustrum hedges with my cordless trimmer after a flush of new growth; bottom left, harvesting comfrey stems to make homemade fertiliser; bottom right, making a hessian sack of comfrey tea to add to our water butt.

A

T

U

U

N

M

Autumn brings transformation.

As autumn arrives in my cottage garden, a subtle shift begins in the hues of foliage from the smoke bush, Japanese acer and our oak tree. Late-flowering perennials, such as *Helianthus* 'Lemon Queen', *Rudbeckia* 'Goldsturm' and *Anemone* 'Wild Swan', decorate the landscape with their welcome blooms, while most other perennials fade into the background and enter into a period of dormancy. Here in Somerset, in the south-west of England, the temperature is mild enough that rose bushes and other shrubs, such as *Weigela* 'Florida Variegata', offer an extra flush of flowers into autumn.

Before dormancy fully takes hold of the garden, there's a final burst of activity with the last harvest of tomatoes (if blight has been successfully avoided), squashes and pumpkins, and the gathering of autumn fruits – raspberries, blackberries and apples. I enjoy these last late delights by baking comforting pies and crumbles.

I make time to observe the plants in the fruit and vegetable garden as their leaves shift from green to amber and red. Strawberry leaves become variegated with warm edges, and the leaves of our blueberry bushes are flushed with maroon.

It's amazing how many edible plants bring an ornamental value to the garden, too, when autumn arrives. The fern-like leaves of our asparagus plants erupt into a vibrant yellow in their raised beds, signalling that it's time to cut them back. I don't rush to do this, and leave them intact in order to enjoy their wonderful colour display for an extra few days.

In the greenhouse, my saffron crocuses (*Crocus sativus L.*) produce delicate purple petals encasing a centre of bright crimson stigmas. These stigmas, when dried, are the saffron that many of us prize and use in our cooking. I harvest them gently with my hands, while leaving

the flower intact. Plucking saffron stigmas in autumn gives me insight into why it is the most expensive spice. My bulbs – I have around 600 – give me about two grams (0.07 ounces) of saffron. But they will give the same amount every year for many years to come, although the squirrels have eaten my entire collection before, so I try to keep the greenhouse windows closed now. The bulbs themselves are inexpensive when ordered from the wholesalers, and the flowers are a great delight: an edible crop that brings me satisfaction through its full lifecycle.

Wildlife friendly

As temperatures fall and daylight hours begin to dwindle, I watch our resident frogs and newts bid farewell to the pond, seeking refuge in the garden for the winter. The ducks undergo a shift too, shedding their feathers as they endure their yearly moult. Their feather-covered enclosure always alarms me when the ducks are mid-moult, but my mind is put at ease as they waddle towards me happily when I open their door in the morning. The ducks look quite straggly in the stage between dropping most of their feathers and before their new ones are fully grown. It is both amusing and adorable. Growing new feathers takes a bit of energy, so it is during this time that the females ease into a period of reduced egg laying, or they may cease to lay at all for a short period. For my partner and me, after a spring and summer of weekly frittatas and scrambled egg breakfasts, the decline in egg production is, honestly, well received. We adopt a new seasonal menu in the kitchen, shifting to soups, stews and other such comfort foods.

In the skies above, hundreds of migrating birds can be seen flying overhead as they respond to the changing seasons. Many of our garden birds are leaving for warmer climates, in search of insects to feast on while supplies are low here. Other species of wintering water birds return to our wetlands.

It is beautiful to watch, but we are also cautious: with this movement of wild birds comes an increased risk of avian flu, and often by the end of autumn our ducks will need to be kept within their pen to keep them healthy. While they are in 'flockdown', we bring them snacks of grass, peas or kale from the garden to keep them entertained. A few of our friends have taken to bringing surplus Halloween pumpkins as a treat for the ducks. They will enjoy these fresh, though sometimes I roast them until they're nice and soft. The ducks seem very grateful for this and I like the sound of their excited quacks when they figure out a pumpkin is on the way.

Later into the season, the brightly coloured leaves of deciduous trees fade and fall to the ground, and a pervasive sense of rest creeps into every corner of the garden, with the occasional evergreen steadfastly carrying on in the background.

Natural mulch After most of the leaves have fallen, I move them out of walkways and lawns and onto the flowerbeds, where they will offer habitats to overwintering creatures, before breaking down and returning nutrients to the soil. Most of the leaves will have fully broken down by the new year, but the oak leaves are tough and rigid and will sometimes remain on the ground until summer. Some gardeners aren't keen on the way this looks, but it's another free mulch, and that's a positive in my eyes.

Towards the end of autumn, a collective sigh of relief accompanies the return of slowness. But as dormancy approaches, the last few weeks of autumn can bring a feeling of sadness for me, as I'm sure they do for many others. I have learned to make space for this feeling. Keeping active in the garden, especially on warmer days, helps me weather it.

Now is the time for bulb planting, which gives me a sense of hope for the next spring. In my first few years in the garden, my bulb planting efforts through autumn were mighty. Now that I have over 10,000 perennial bulbs settled into the ground, my planting schedule is a bit more relaxed. I'm mainly topping things up here or there according to what I felt was missing in spring, and trying out the odd new variety of tulip. I will always plant something in autumn for the hopeful experience and pleasure of the process. Once those final spring-flowering bulbs are in the soil, it's time to surrender into a well-deserved rest.

Hopeful bulb planting

The first naturalised bulb project I started in our garden was the crocus lawn. In our second autumn in the cottage, I added between 600 to 800 Pickwick crocus bulbs to one particular area of grass, one at a time with a small bulb planter. It took quite a long time to plant them in this way, and my next-door neighbour regularly checked on me when I was crouched over the grass in my waterproofs and it was belting down with rain. Every few days she would appear over the garden fence and ask for my running total, and offer me some words of encouragement. The planting project spanned most of a year and by the time the crocuses flowered in March, the process had blossomed into a social rhythm I enjoyed as much as seeing the flowers. I was glad to share the delight of them appearing across the lawn with my neighbour.

The way I work with my garden is often inspired by the people and places that are important to me. I started growing bulbs beyond formal borders and in my grass, creating my crocus lawn, to emulate what I had seen in one of my favourite places to visit, The Courts Garden in Holt, Wiltshire. I try to visit this garden at the end of every winter or start of spring to see their crocus collection. Why not create a version at home? I've loved seeing others recreate my crocus lawn in their spaces – including in pots and window boxes. The joy of these flowers is transferable to any space.

Cultivating a crocus lawn

Crocus lawns are often planted with early flowering varieties of crocus such as *Crocus tommasinianus* or *Crocus sieberi*. I decided to plant mine with a Dutch variety of crocus called 'Pickwick', which flowers slightly later than other crocuses and has larger flowers. The larger flowers meant that I wouldn't have to plant as many bulbs to build an impressive purple display. I've included my methods for planting later in this section (see page 162).

After a couple of years of growing the crocus lawn, once I felt confident that it had enough bulbs and was more or less self-sufficient, I moved on to my next naturalising project – my mini meadow. This is a smaller

Above: crocus bulbs and a small bulb planter. Opposite: top left, loosening sections of turf with a spade; top right, gently lifting the loosened turf to expose the soil; bottom left, positioning crocus bulbs into the soil; bottom right, gently pushing the turf back into position after planting.

area of lawn we have under an oak tree. Spring-flowering bulbs work really well here because of the light levels. In the summer the lawn is shaded by the tree above. In spring, however, the oak hasn't yet produced its leaves and so there is more available light for flowers to grow below. I had seen a collection of wood anemones, daffodils and snake's head fritillaries naturalised in the grass at Iford Manor in Wiltshire, and this assortment of bulbs (coupled with my dad's love of wild fritillary meadows) inspired the planting of my own mini meadow.

I learned from planting my crocus lawn that individual bulb planting takes a lot of time and energy, so this time I decided to completely remove the turf from the planting area, and add the bulbs into the exposed soil in a much denser pattern. This method came with a messy aftermath of mud for a couple of weeks, but by spring there was a high-impact miniature meadow in bloom.

Compared to growing bulbs formally in a border, there is a beautiful wild look to naturalised bulbs. The green backdrop of grasses and mosses provides a wonderful and natural contrast to the vivid pops of purple in crocuses and snake's head fritillaries. I especially love moss for this reason; it has a soft, spongy texture and a lime green colour that looks so fresh and wild. There is a symbolism to how curation (the crocuses) meets wilderness (the moss) in my garden; I love how these two elements can harmonise together to create something beautiful.

Sometimes, my bulb planting drifts into winter if I'm not feeling very organised. The bulbs may flower a week or so later if they are planted in winter, but it's still worth getting them in the ground. I often find myself longing for something constructive to do outside when the main gardening window is over. Bulb planting brings a fantastic sense of energy and momentum for me, and then once those bulbs are in the ground I am given a hope and excitement to carry me through winter while I wait for the rewards of spring.

I'm looking at our spring garden now, and most of the borders and lawns have some sort of perennial bulb growing in them. I don't like to grow many bulbs that will only flower once, because it feels wasteful. And yet the autumn bulb planting is a seasonal rhythm I depend on. Most of what goes in will stay there for years to come, building on the planting of the previous years rather than replacing it. In my mind, this means the garden just gets better and better. Every spring the garden looks fuller, and I imagine that I will soon run out of space, once I have naturalised (see page 158) as much of the lawn as is practical (while leaving some walkways and places for ducks and dogs to use). My plan is to volunteer in our village and plant up some of the banks and roundabouts, and share the joy of spring flowers beyond my own garden.

WHY PLANT BULBS?

Bulbs bring us an entire additional layer to our growing spaces. In the lawn, we may well not grow anything more than grass, and perhaps some dandelions, daisies or clover through the warmer times of year. By planting bulbs in autumn, we introduce a whole new layer of colour and joy for ourselves in late winter or early spring, and we provide food for early pollinators too. As our winters become increasingly mild, insects are active earlier, and our native plants may not be able to provide a food source for them quite as early as they require. By planting early-flowering bulbs such as snowdrops and crocuses, we offer an extended period of pollen and nectar for them, helping them to weather the most difficult time of year. We can also add bulbs to borders and pots, where they are able to grow around our existing perennial plants.

- When choosing bulbs to grow in a lawn, you will want to look for varieties that naturalise well. This means that over the years they will spread, and your collection should be sustained for years to come.

- You should also consider the sunlight exposure of your planting site, and whether the area is particularly wet or dry. Tulips, for example, prefer **full sun**, and are likely to rot in wet soil. Though most tulips are unlikely to spread, if you meet their ideal growing conditions, they can rebloom for many years with success. Snake's head fritillaries, on the other hand, prefer dappled shade and wetter soil conditions.

You can do a bit of trial and error in your garden before you commit to large scale planting. Pop a small assortment of bulbs in various areas of the garden and watch how they perform and reflower over a year or two. Sometimes the garden's plan may be at odds with our own. I have one border where I would love to grow tulips, but after three failed attempts I have come to accept that it is just too damp. Instead, I will try growing snake's head fritillaries.

- Another consideration when it comes to selecting bulbs, particularly if you are planting them in a lawn, is flowering time. Keep in mind that you won't be able to mow the grass over the bulbs for six weeks after they have flowered. For earlier blooming varieties like snowdrops, this might not affect your mowing schedule at all. The grass will still be short once the snowdrop leaves have finished their growth cycle. For later flowering varieties like daffodils or camassia, allowing time for their leaves to grow may get in the way of your lawn mowing schedule.

- Dainty plants with earlier flowering times generally look better naturalised in lawns. The earlier flowering times mean the surrounding grass will be shorter, and so the lawn will still look quite tidy. For this type of planting, you might choose from snowdrops, crocuses, smaller varieties of daffodils, wood anemones, muscari or snake's head fritillaries.

- Taller flowers with a later flowering time look best in longer, more wild areas of grass. This includes taller varieties of daffodils, camassias, alliums and crown imperial fritillaries. Some gardeners plant tall tulips in long meadows of grass too. Though these displays will lessen over the years rather than spreading, they can look very impressive and quite unusual.

- There are colour and aesthetic decisions to make, too. Larger flowers generally produce larger leaves after they have flowered, so they can make lawns look very leafy once your display has finished. Consider which colours you like, and whether you want to mix colours together. I prefer to grow crocuses in a mass of one variety, whereas other gardeners prefer to mix types together and create a colourful tapestry effect. It can be helpful to make a mock colour scheme before ordering your bulbs. I like to cut out photos from garden catalogues and arrange them together on a page to see how particular combinations feel.

- Once you've planted potentially hundreds or thousands of bulbs in the lawn, it is much harder to remove them again, so it's worth taking your time over the selection process. This can be fun and expressive, and a chance to play with colour and form.

The bulbs I grow in my garden are as follows, in order of flowering time. All of these were planted in autumn or early winter, with the intention of lasting for many years to come.

BULB	LOCATION	SUN EXPOSURE IN MY GARDEN	DOES IT NATURALISE?
Galanthus nivalis (common snowdrop)	Border near cottage	Semi-shade	Yes
Galanthus woronowii (snowdrop with large, green leaves)	Naturalised in mini-meadow lawn and lawn around pond	Semi-shade	Yes
Iris reticulata (assorted variety)	Borders near shed	Semi-shade	Yes
'Firefly' crocus	Naturalised in lawn around pond	Full sun	Yes
'Jeanne d'Arc' crocus	Naturalised in lawn around greenhouse	Full sun	Yes
'Pickwick' crocus	Naturalised in crocus lawn	Full sun	Yes
Muscari 'Baby's Breath' and *azureum*	Borders along fences	Semi-shade	Yes
Narcissus 'Ice Follies'	Naturalised in long grass in orchard	Full sun	Yes
Narcissus 'Pueblo' (Jonquilla)	Naturalised in mini-meadow lawn	Partial sun	Yes

BULB	LOCATION	SUN EXPOSURE IN MY GARDEN	DOES IT NATURALISE?
Fritillaria meleagris (snake's head fritillary)	Naturalised in mini-meadow lawn	Partial sun	Yes
Anemone nemorosa 'Alba' (woodland anemone)	Naturalised in mini-meadow lawn	Partial sun	Yes – slowly
Wild garlic	Borders around pond	Semi-shade	Yes
Bluebell	Borders around pond, fences, and naturalised in long grass in the orchard	Semi-shade	Yes
Tulip 'Design impression'	Borders around greenhouse	Full sun	Perennial but doesn't spread
Tulip 'Ivory Floradale'	Borders around greenhouse	Full sun	Perennial but doesn't spread
Tulip 'Peppermint Stick' (botanical tulip)	Border along polytunnel	Partial sun	Yes
Allium 'Mount Everest'	Borders around greenhouse	Full sun	Perennial and can be spread via division but will not naturalise

PLANTING BULBS IN THE LAWN

My own experiences and experiments have led me to a few tried-and-tested methods when it comes to planting mini meadows.

- A general rule of thumb is to plant bulbs in a hole as deep as three times their height (and deeper still if you feel they are at risk of being dug up by wildlife). Ideally, the pointy end of the bulb points skyward, which helps guide new shoots towards the light. But nature is adaptable; if some bulbs land on their side or find themselves a bit askew, they will cope just fine.

- The ideal time to plant your bulbs is during the autumn months, from late September to November. This timing allows the bulbs to establish their roots before the winter frost sets in, ensuring they're ready to burst into life come spring. However, if autumn escapes you, don't fret; planting can continue into winter, provided the ground isn't frozen. Bulbs planted later may bloom a bit later in the season or spend their first year building a strong foundation, showing their full potential in the following spring. Remember, patience in gardening often reaps the most beautiful rewards.

- A bulb planter can be useful. In my experience, anything fewer than one or two hundred bulbs is achievable with a bulb planter. Small bulb planters are available for things like snowdrop and crocus bulbs, and larger ones are better suited to sturdier bulbs such as daffodils and alliums. It is easiest to use a bulb planter when the ground is wet, so if possible, opt for planting after a spell of rain. If back strain is a concern, long-handled bulb planters offer a solution, allowing you to work standing up, thereby easing the load on your back.

- When planning the number of bulbs per square metre for naturalising in your lawn, it's essential to strike a balance between creating a dense, vibrant display and allowing enough space for each plant to thrive and multiply over the years. For smaller bulbs like crocuses, snowdrops and muscari, which tend to be less intrusive and can create a beautiful carpet of colour, planting around 150–200 bulbs per square metre is advised. This density ensures a visually impactful display while still leaving room for the bulbs to spread and naturalise over time. Larger bulbs, such as daffodils, require more space due to their size and the larger foliage they produce. For these, a planting density of 25–30 bulbs per square metre works well. This arrangement allows for the bulbs to be planted in drifts, which creates a natural and aesthetically pleasing appearance as they grow and bloom.

- If you are planting hundreds of bulbs and aiming for a strong display in the first year of flowering, individual planting with a bulb planter might not be the best approach. Instead, using a spade, I remove sections of turf from the entire area designated for the mini meadow. I tackle individual rectangles at a time, each roughly 30cm (12in) in height and 60cm (24in) in width, and

about 10cm (4in) deep, though this depth should be adjusted to suit the specific bulbs being planted. Care is taken to lift the turf gently, trying to keep it as intact as possible. Then, I position my bulbs within the bare earth beneath. After the bulbs are snugly placed in their new homes, the turf is carefully repositioned, and pressed down firmly to ensure good contact with the soil beneath. I've found that standing on the edges of the replaced sections helps to secure them in place, serving as an effective deterrent against curious squirrels looking for a snack. At first, the seams of the replaced turf may appear quite muddy. However, within a few weeks, these signs of disturbance begin to vanish, and by spring, you will be rewarded with a densely planted mini meadow, teeming with life and bursting with colour.

Planting bulbs in pots

Those without a physical garden can still grow bulbs in pots, and may be pleasantly surprised by how many you can squeeze into a single pot using the 'lasagne' planting method. This technique involves layering different types of bulbs at various depths to ensure a long-lasting display of blooms. The great thing about growing bulbs in pots is that there is room for experimentation: you might choose bulbs that flower all at once, or you can create a more staggered display with a layer of early-flowering snowdrops, followed by daffodils, and then finally tulips at the end of spring. These bulbs can be dug out of the pot and stored in a dark, dry place for later reuse, or left in situ in their pots and tucked away for the remainder of the year.

Begin by placing larger bulbs like alliums at the bottom of the pot, planting them about 20cm (8in) deep, and then top this with a layer of soil or compost. The next layer should consist of medium-sized bulbs such as daffodils, which are set around 12cm (5in) deep. After covering this layer with soil or compost, add smaller bulbs like snowdrops and crocuses to the top layer, planting them about 7.5cm (3in) deep. Ensure each bulb is spaced a few inches apart from its neighbours to give them room to expand and grow.

To prevent the bulbs from becoming waterlogged, it's crucial to ensure good drainage. Opt for a pot with drainage holes and consider adding a layer of gravel or broken pottery at the bottom before filling it with soil. This setup helps water flow smoothly and keeps the bulbs healthy.

Once your bulbs are in place, top the soil with a layer of moss. This not only retains moisture, helping to create a stable environment for the bulbs, but it also adds a lush, natural aesthetic to your pot. When considering the placement of your mini meadow, find a spot where it will receive enough sunlight. Some shade is acceptable and can still result in blooms, although too much shade may lead to smaller flowers that bloom later in the season. If you're growing your bulbs indoors, keep the soil consistently moist, especially if indoor heating is on, as this can dry out the soil quickly. For outdoor pots, placing them where they can be rained on usually means you won't need to manually water them, unless there's a prolonged dry spell.

A note on pests

Adding bulbs to the garden can attract wild visitors that want to feast on your hard work. Squirrels, deer and rabbits can be particularly fond of bulbs. We are very lucky in our garden, and apart from the odd squirrel pinching a tulip here or there, we tend to manage. If you do find that wild creatures are a problem, here are a few strategies can help protect your plantings:

- **Mesh**
  Covering your planted areas with a wire mesh can physically block larger pests from digging up bulbs. This strategy works really well if you are growing in pots. Simply cover the soil surface or top of the pot with wire mesh, either burying the edges in the soil or securing them to the edge of the pot.

- **Chilli powder**
  Sprinkling chilli powder around planting sites can deter squirrels due to their sensitive noses. This strategy only works in the short term, and the powder should be reapplied after rain.

- **Deeper planting**
  Planting bulbs deeper than recommended can make it harder work for pests to reach them. In our garden, I plant tulips two or three times deeper than general guidelines. They still flower well.

- **Choose wisely**
  Some bulbs, like daffodils and alliums, are naturally resistant to pests. If rabbits or squirrels are a known problem in your garden, consider focusing on these less appetizing options when you are selecting your bulbs.

Meadow upkeep

Ensuring your mini meadow continues to thrive and evolve over the years requires a gentle touch and a bit of patience. The secret lies in knowing when to step back and let nature take its course.

Resist the urge to mow the grass too soon after the last flowers have bid their farewells. We wait about six weeks before we mow the lawn again – ideally the leaves will have faded and started to die back before mowing. Bulbs are vessels of stored energy, so allowing the leaves to photosynthesise, grow and die back naturally means the plant can gather and store as much energy in its bulbs as it can, in turn feeding next year's display.

As the seasons pass, you'll witness the naturalisation process at work; many bulb species are designed by nature to multiply and spread via seed or undergrown bulb division. These processes will gradually fill out your mini meadow, creating a denser, more vibrant tapestry of colour and life.

The ever-evolving landscape is part of the charm of a mini meadow, with its ability to surprise and grow more beautiful with time. It's wise to conduct an annual review of your meadow's progress and to assess the balance of your mini ecosystem. Some areas may become overcrowded, necessitating a gentle intervention to lift and divide clumps of bulbs. You might notice dense patches of leaves with few flowers during the spring flowering period; this is a good indicator that it's time to divide the bulbs. Alternatively, if you want to help a single patch of flowers cover a wider area in the garden – especially for bulbs that are slower to spread, like snowdrops – you can lift the bulbs for this purpose too. A good time to lift and divide your bulbs is after the flowering period has finished, while the leaves are still green. For smaller, shallower bulbs like muscari, bluebells or snowdrops, gently use a hand trowel to lift the bulbs from the soil, ensuring to keep the leaves attached. The leaves help provide energy to the bulbs as they establish in their new location. Larger bulbs like daffodils will be planted a bit deeper, so it is best to use a spade to dig them out without damaging the bulbs. Once you have pulled up a mass of bulbs, gently separate these with your hands. Replant the bulbs in smaller groups around the garden, spacing them about 10cm (4in) apart. Next year, you will be rewarded with a broader flowering area.

In areas that have gaps, it may be time to introduce new bulbs to rejuvenate and maintain the display's vibrancy. I keep a notebook of 'strong' and 'weak' areas in my bulb displays, and document these through photos so I can reference back in my next autumn of planting. This cycle of care and observation ensures that your mini meadow not only endures but flourishes, becoming a source of joy and beauty for years to come.

Growing everlasting tulips

I've always held a particular fondness for tulips, and long before I took up gardening myself, I would admire them in public parks and gardens. It was initially disheartening to discover that tulips are commonly treated as annuals (flowers and bulbs to be discarded after a single season's bloom and replaced with new ones). This practice seemed expensive and wasteful, considering the years of cultivation each bulb undergoes before it even enters our gardens – all seemingly for a fleeting display of beauty.

I learned more and discovered that certain varieties are capable of blooming for successive years when left undisturbed in the soil, with some even able to multiply. Additionally, there are specific planting and care techniques that can help ensure treasured tulips remain vibrant and healthy.

Tulips can be planted at any time during the autumn or up to the first half of winter. Now, with most of my tulip bulbs well-established in the ground – many of which have been thriving for five years or more – I dedicate each autumn to replenishing any gaps in the display. These gaps might occur where bulbs have been accidentally damaged during border maintenance, particularly when digging spaces for new perennials and shrubs (see page 64). This annual ritual of topping up bulbs ensures that the vibrant spectacle of my tulips continues unabated.

Choosing bulbs

The key to a lasting tulip display lies in the choice of species. Among my favoured varieties – which multiply in number once you have planted them – are 'Bakeri', 'Lady Jane' and 'Peppermint Stick', each boasting their own unique charm. Additionally, Viridiflora tulips, Darwin hybrids, Fosteriana and Kaufmanniana cultivars have proven themselves reliable performers in my garden. Though these varieties will not spread, they generously reflower for a number of years. Some of my favourite choices are 'Spring Green', 'Ivory Floradale' and 'Pink Impression'.

Plant deep

Depth of planting is a pivotal factor in the longevity of tulips. Many of my tulip bulbs have been planted 25cm (10in) into the soil. A deeper burial serves as a deterrent to pests and mitigates the risk of the bulbs splitting. Shallow planting encourages the bulbs to multiply by division; this natural process involves the original bulb producing smaller bulbs or 'offsets' from its base, which can eventually grow into new plants. However, these new bulbs are often undersized and may produce only foliage, not flowers, in their initial years.
A deeper resting place ensures the nourishment of a singular bulb over an extended period, favouring the blossoming of magnificent flowers over proliferation.

Place carefully

Success with tulips also hinges on their placement. They thrive under conditions of dry summers and well-draining soil, which protect them from rot, and require lots of sunlight to flourish. Furthermore, a cold winter is crucial for their reflowering, making the selection of their location a matter of paramount importance. I have found in my garden that the best way to get this right is through trial and error, so don't be put off if your first attempts don't feel successful.

Post-flowering care

The care tulips receive after blooming significantly impacts their ability to return in the following year. It is wise to remove the seedheads from the stems after the petals have faded or fallen away, and while the leaves are still green. I simply snap the seedhead from the top of the stem using my fingers, and discard this onto the soil to break down. If you are more particular about keeping the tulip plants tidy, you can snip the entire stem from the base of the plant with a pair of secateurs, leaving only the leaves in place. It is important to remove the seedheads while the leaves are still green, because this is when the plant is collecting energy via photosynthesis, and diverting it back into bulb for seed production. Removing the seedheads means the plant won't spend energy producing seed, and will instead store energy in its bulb for next year's growth.

Providing nutrients through organic means, such as seaweed fertiliser or homemade comfrey tea (see images on page 138), after the tulip flowers have finished and while the leaves are still green can be useful. I must admit though, I am not usually organised enough to do this, and I find that as long as my soil is healthy that is enough to keep the bulbs well fed. A no-dig approach and regular mulching with organic matter (see page 127) are usually enough to ensure that the soil is nourished and balanced.

Leave the tulip leaves in place until they turn brown and crispy, signalling the end of photosynthesis and the storage of energy within the bulb for the next year's bloom. Once the leaves have turned brown, they can be left in situ to break down naturally, or gently detached from the bulb with a little tug, if you'd like to tidy them up.

Planting edible bulbs

My love of planting bulbs in autumn extends to the vegetable garden, too. In the middle of the season, I will add around 50 garlic cloves to the raised beds and polytunnel with a bulb planter. I have tried planting a few varieties of garlic over the years, but my absolute favourite is elephant garlic for the novelty of its size. The bulbs are much larger than other types of garlic and are usually about 10cm (4in) wide. The flavour of the cloves is milder than other garlics, and their large size makes them great for roasting. Autumn varieties of onions and shallots can also be planted from sets (small bulbs) in the autumn, though I don't tend to grow these now that my perennial onion patch is well-established.

Growing with nature

Our gardens, and much of the wildlife that inhabit them, transition into dormancy in autumn. During this time, there are things we can do to help support them through this change, including protecting the microorganisms in our soil and creating larger habitats for hedgehogs and mice.

Mulching with autumn leaves

Although it feels as though the best of autumn has finished once the colourful trees have faded and dropped their leaves, these fallen leaves are a hugely valuable resource for our soil. Instead of removing fallen leaves from your garden, repurpose them into mulch or leaf mould. One common method involves gathering the leaves into bins or plastic bags, where over time, they break down into leaf mould. This process transforms the leaves into a nutrient-dense organic material by the following year, which is excellent for enriching the soil in garden beds or improving potting mixes for potted plants.

Personally, I prefer to leave the leaves in place, except those on the lawn. To prevent the grass underneath from becoming sludgy and damaged, I use a leaf blower to move the leaves onto the flower beds. There, they decompose naturally, enriching the soil as they break down. The decomposition rate varies depending on the leaf type: smaller, thinner leaves from trees like damson and Japanese maple break down within a few months, while thicker leaves, such as those from oak trees, can remain on the soil surface until the following spring. I regularly notice ladybirds, caterpillars and other small insects under these sturdy leaves, and I take this as a positive sign, indicating that the leaf layer is beneficial to the garden's natural ecosystem.

There are a number of advantages when it comes to applying a leaf mulch directly to the soil surface. The seasonal cycle of deciduous trees helps to redistribute nutrients across layers of earth. The expansive root systems of trees pull nutrients from deeper layers of our soil, and after these leaves fall in autumn, they decay into the soil surface. As these leaves break down, the nutrients are returned to shallow layers of soil, where they can be utilised by plants with smaller root systems, including our beloved perennials and vegetables. Leaf mulch also offers protection against extreme weather conditions, including frost, and helps prevent soil erosion caused by wind and rain.

If you prefer to make leaf mould by transferring leaves into compost bins or plastic bags, the resulting organic material is incredibly nutrient-rich and can be used the following year as a top dressing for the soil or as mulch around potted plants. Leaf mould is particularly beneficial around plants that naturally grow in the understory of woodlands, such as ferns, as it closely replicates their native growing conditions.

Hibernation spots for hedgehogs and other creatures

As temperatures begin to drop, the shift into colder months prompts a variety of wildlife species to start their hibernation process. Among these, hedgehogs, bats, dormice, squirrels, snails, newts, frogs and various insects seek refuge to sleep through the winter. This natural cycle highlights the importance of providing accessible, sheltered places for these creatures to hibernate safely.

Supporting hibernating wildlife involves a conscious effort to leave parts of the garden in a more natural, undisturbed state. For smaller creatures such as newts and insects, creating stacks of stones, twigs, logs and piles of leaves can offer the perfect hibernation spots. These simple habitats can be easily integrated into garden spaces, often going unnoticed but serving as crucial sanctuaries for garden wildlife. In my own garden, I've observed insects taking shelter within the leaf mulch layer, and toads or newts finding refuge in or around our compost bins.

Larger creatures, including hedgehogs, tend to seek out more substantial hiding places such as old rabbit burrows, tree roots, nooks under sheds and outbuildings, or nesting under hedgerows. For those looking to actively support these animals, constructing or purchasing hedgehog houses from sheet wood can provide a dedicated space for them to hibernate. Alternatively, enhancing the garden's natural environment to suit their needs is equally beneficial. My approach has been to offer natural hibernation spots by relocating old logs beneath our hedges. Whenever trees are cut or pruned, instead of disposing of the excess wood, I arrange stacks of logs under the hedges. While these may be almost invisible to us, they become invaluable habitats for a variety of wildlife seeking shelter.

Sowing green manure

I like to 'overwinter' crops such as kale, chard, garlic and broad beans (sowing vegetable seeds in autumn, and then keeping these plants in the soil until they crop in spring – see page 84). These overwintering plants won't put on a lot of growth through the coldest months, and they may look slightly small and uneven outside of their peak growing window, but they keep my soil full and busy instead of leaving it empty. I am comfortable with my growing space looking a little uneven through winter, and the benefits of keeping life in the soil feel well worth it for me, but those who like to keep their gardens very tidy may prefer to simply mulch their soil with a layer of compost instead.

After the main growing season, when we clear away spent crops like tomatoes, beans and squashes, is the time to sow seed mixes, known as green manure, to bring structure back where soil is depleted and empty.

These seed mixes, designed to enrich the soil, can be sown at the beginning of autumn. By the time spring arrives, these plants are ready to be cut down, or 'chopped and dropped', allowing their foliage to decompose naturally on the soil surface. This process not only returns valuable nutrients to the earth but also improves soil structure and fertility, making it a prime growing medium for the next planting season.

Green manures include a variety of plants such as clover, field beans, rye and grasses, each selected for their ability to contribute positively to the soil's health. After the green manure has decomposed into the ground, the soil is ready to support edible plants once more.

Selective cutting back

As perennial plants and shrubs in our borders enter dormancy, the instinct to tidy up by cutting back dead foliage can feel strong. However, I think it's important to consider the ecological benefits of leaving some of this growth in place. Dead stems can provide vital shelter for insects such as ladybirds throughout the winter months, while seeds and rosehips offer essential food sources for birds.

There are instances, of course, where cutting back is necessary for the health of the garden. For example, this is the time to remove asparagus foliage to help prevent asparagus beetle infestations. Some perennial plants such as hostas and peonies need cutting back to prevent them from becoming sludgy.

Other dead or dormant plants, particularly those that remain sturdy throughout the winter – such as woody perennials like echinacea or helianthus, summer clematis and shrubs like hydrangeas – can be left untouched, or unpruned, until the start of spring. These plants not only provide structural interest in the garden during the colder months but also continue to support the garden's biodiversity.

Feeding the birds

From autumn, birds that do not migrate ahead of winter face the challenge of finding sufficient food. Fatty foods become increasingly crucial for their survival as we head towards and through winter. A practical way to support them during these times is by topping up bird feeders with a variety of bird-friendly food. In autumn, a mix of seeds and grains is perfect for a broad range of birds. As the season progresses into winter, it's beneficial to shift focus towards higher fat foods like suet, fat balls and peanuts, which provide the concentrated energy birds need to maintain their body heat in freezing conditions. Berries and other fruits can also be offered to attract a variety of species that may benefit from these natural food sources.

Birds rely on natural sources of food in our gardens, such as insects, berries and seeds. By consciously choosing not to remove certain natural resources, we provide a vital food supply. In my garden, I always leave rosehips in place through autumn and winter. These rosehips are particularly popular with blackbirds and thrushes, offering them a significant source of nutrients. Leaving a leaf mulch on the soil has proven beneficial for sustaining insect populations. It's not uncommon to observe robins rustling through the fallen leaves in search of insects to eat.

Ivy is another plant that I allow to flourish in the garden due to its late-ripening berries, which provide an abundant food source for birds when few other resources are available. Similarly, if sunflowers have been a part of the summer garden, I make it a point to leave a few standing after their bright yellow petals have gone. The seeds of sunflowers are an energy-dense, excellent food source for birds and squirrels.

Watching the colourful autumn borders flower

When my gardening journey began, I eagerly filled my borders with cottage garden classics like roses, foxgloves and delphiniums. The result was stunning, until autumn arrived and most of the blooms had faded. This led me on to the subsequent aim of introducing a collection of autumn-flowering perennials among the summer favourites. It's an evolving project, as many things in my garden are, but each year my autumn garden grows more vibrant as these plants establish.

It is more of a challenge to keep the garden looking good through autumn and into winter. In that challenge, though, there is reward, and I am very appreciative of colourful asters and echinacea as we bid farewell to the main growing seasons. I find that autumn-flowering perennials are best planted in spring, when the weather is still cool enough that it won't stress new plants, and there are a number of months for the plants to establish themselves. This time to establish should mean you get a few flowers within the first year of growing. If you have missed the spring window for planting, though, autumn is a great second choice for hardy perennials, which should weather the colder months and reward you with growth and blooms in the following year (see page 77).

I spend a bit of time weeding the borders through autumn. I'm not too meticulous about this, but it helps keep the weeds in check ahead of next year. We get a lot of creeping buttercups in our garden, and although they are lovely flowers, their tendency to spread can overwhelm other plants. I usually weed by using my hands to lightly pull up small seedlings, tearing them up and leaving them to break down on the soil surface. For taprooted weeds, such as dandelions or unwanted cow parsley, I use a long metal rod that helps pry out the deep roots individually. I compost taprooted weeds because sometimes they resprout on the soil surface if left in the 'chop and drop' fashion, but in the compost heap, they will decay under the warm and dark conditions. I don't remove all weeds, as they are often beneficial to wildlife and can be quite beautiful in their own right if we overcome the way we have been taught to view them. My strategy is to prevent them from overcrowding the more designed areas of my garden and to let them run wild in the designated wildlife areas.

Autumn weeding

Helianthus 'Lemon Queen'

Perennial sunflowers, such as 'Lemon Queen', bring fabulous height and vibrant yellow to the garden in autumn. They prefer a sunny spot at the back of the border, where their long stems can sway gracefully in the wind. I've found that leaving the foliage intact over autumn and winter offers a protective habitat for hibernating insects. These plants are typically bought as potted specimens and thrive in well-drained soil, adding a burst of late-season colour and life to the garden. I introduced two medium pots to the garden a couple of years ago, and I have been really impressed with how much the plants have spread already.

Echinacea

Echinacea's long flowering period makes it a standout front-of-border plant, ideal for planting in sunny positions. While they can be grown from seed, buying potted plants accelerates establishment. The cone-shaped flowers come in a variety of colours, but I'm particularly fond of the white-petaled varieties like 'White Swan' for their soft, delicate appearance. Plant them in well-drained soil and full sun to encourage a robust display that complements the rich tones of autumn foliage.

Rudbeckia 'Goldsturm'

Rudbeckia, with its easy growth from seed and appeal to pollinators, is a must-have for the autumn garden. A sunny spot is essential for these golden-yellow flowers to thrive. I sowed a packet of 'Goldsturm' rudbeckia seeds, and after a couple of years of care in the greenhouse, I was rewarded with 60 vibrant plants from a single packet of seeds. They require moderately fertile, well-drained soil and benefit from occasional watering during dry spells, ensuring a spectacular display each year.

Hydrangea paniculata 'Limelight'

Hydrangeas are exceptionally useful shrubs. They have a long flowering season, and will live happily in full sun or partial shade. I have some areas of the garden that are quite heavily shaded, and hydrangeas still bring us blooms. A favourite of mine is the 'Limelight' hydrangea, with its shifting hues from lime green at the start of summer, to cream in midsummer, and finally to warm pink as we move into autumn. These plants provide a versatile and evolving display across many months.

Hydrangeas are an excellent choice for adding structure to the middle or back of a border. Plant in rich, moist soil and consider leaving the dried flowers on the plant through winter for added interest.

Saffron crocuses

Saffron crocuses offer both ornamental beauty and practical harvests. Plant the bulbs at the end of summer in a sunny, well-drained spot for blooms each autumn. They are a welcome sight in the garden if you are a fan of spring crocus displays. Saffron crocuses have delicate purple flowers and bright orange stamens that can be harvested and dried. I grow mine in my greenhouse, to protect them from bad weather. Last year I planted 700 bulbs in the large greenhouse underneath our agave and cacti. They looked beautiful at the beginning of autumn; however, to my disappointment, I left the windows open and a squirrel ate every last bulb. As a devoted fan of crocuses, I will be trying again next autumn.

Japanese anemones

Japanese anemones offer a wonderfully long flowering season, from May to November. Their ability to spread and adapt makes them invaluable for filling garden gaps. Plant in fertile, well-drained soil, and they will tolerate some shade, making them versatile for various garden spots. Their diverse heights and flower forms, from single to double petals, offer dynamic visual interest. A favourite variety of mine is 'Wild Swan', a single-petalled anemone with a white front and soft purple colour on its reverse. These flowers look beautiful when they sway in the wind, with the movement revealing flecks of purple. Another variety I grow in our garden is 'Frilly Knickers', a double-petalled anemone with a very soft hint of purple colouring. The frilly petals remind me of plants I would grow in summer, and so it feels the warmer seasons are extended.

Asters

Asters inject a final flourish of colour into the autumn garden with their tall, upright stems and daisy-like flowers ranging from white to purple to pink. Varieties like 'Mönch' provide a pop of purple at about 1m (3.3ft) tall, ideal for the middle or back of the border. Plant in fertile, well-drained soil in full sun to maximise their flowering potential. Asters look especially beautiful after rain, with water droplets enhancing their natural beauty, making them a joyful sight in the autumn landscape.

Penstemon 'Sour Grapes'

Penstemon 'Sour Grapes' is an invaluable addition to the autumn garden, offering a splash of colour with its distinctive bluish-purple flowers that can extend the floral display into the cooler months. This perennial prefers a sunny spot in the garden and thrives in well-drained soil. From my own experience, 'Sour Grapes' not only adds visual interest but also attracts a variety of pollinators, making it an excellent choice for a wildlife-friendly garden. Deadheading spent blooms can encourage a longer flowering period, extending the enjoyment of its vibrant colours into autumn.

Agastache

Agastache, with its aromatic foliage and spikes of tubular flowers, is a standout plant that brings both scent and colour to the late summer and autumn garden. Available in shades of orange, pink and purple, agastache is particularly drought-tolerant once established, making it a low-maintenance choice for sunny borders. Agastache was one of the first plants I introduced to our garden five years ago after picking up a couple of plants in our local farmer's market. I've since found that its nectar-rich flowers are a magnet for bees and butterflies. Plant agastache in full sun and well-drained soil to promote vigorous growth and abundant blooms. Cutting back the flower stems after blooming can help maintain a tidy appearance and encourage further flowering.

Jerusalem artichoke flowers

While Jerusalem artichokes (*Helianthus tuberosus*) are often grown for their edible tubers, their flowers are a delightful bonus, resembling small sunflowers and adding a bright, sunny aspect to the garden in late summer to autumn. These tall plants can reach heights of up to 3m (9.8ft). They prefer a sunny position in the garden and are tolerant of most soil types, though they thrive in fertile, well-drained soil. It's worth noting that they can spread vigorously, so consider their placement carefully or contain their growth to prevent them from overtaking other plants.

Sowing seeds

Seed sowing is substantially slower in autumn due to falling temperatures and lower levels of light, but it doesn't have to stop completely. Personally, I really enjoy seed sowing in autumn because there is a simplicity and slowness to it when compared to the rush of seed sowing in spring. Some seeds will grow and give food with relative immediacy. Many of the crops we sow in autumn will grow gently through the colder months of the year before giving us their main harvest the following spring. They offer me a reassurance that the seasons will cycle through their rhythm as they always do, and warmer days will eventually return.

The start of autumn is a good time to fill in any gaps around the vegetable garden with various new seeds, ensuring you don't have exposed and empty soil between the main growing periods.

Edible plants I love sowing cavolo nero kale and various varieties of chard to plug any empty spots in the raised beds or polytunnel. Sown at the start of autumn, they will grow through the season to fill the space and create harvests, and keep going through to spring. I grow them with an aesthetic appreciation, too. Chard leaves are a beautiful limey green, reminiscent of fresh spring growth, while their stems can be almost neon in colour. Peppermint chard in particular has wonderful pink stems. I grow cavolo nero and am ever in awe of its amazing towering structure as it grows taller, and its leaves have a fascinating bubbly texture.

Other edible plants to sow from seed have a shorter, quicker growing cycle, so can be sown at the start of autumn and deliver food in the same season: spinach, dill, mizuna and pak choi.

I take time to sow my late autumn-sown broad bean seeds as they sit patiently in the soil, waiting for their time to shine next year. They remind me not to ask too much of myself during these shorter days.

Soil health

Broad beans are also nitrogen fixers, meaning they have the ability to convert atmospheric nitrogen into a form that plants can use, enriching the soil without the need for chemical fertilisers. This makes them particularly beneficial to get into the soil to rejuvenate it after a summer of growing fruit and vegetable plants. I sow a variety called 'Aquadulce Claudia' and look forward to an early and robust crop at the start of spring.

Hardy annuals such as sweet peas and cornflowers can be sown in autumn to provide a head start in the following year. Sowing these flowers in the cooler months allows for a more established root system and earlier blooming. I find that sweet peas, in particular, will benefit from the colder start, resulting in stronger, more vigorous plants that are ready to climb and cascade with their fragrant blooms as soon as the summer returns. Cornflowers, with their delightful blue hues, will add a splash of colour at the end of spring, brightening up the garden and attracting pollinators.

For those who are short on either the space to sow autumn seeds or the time to do so, small plug plants from a local garden center are a good option, especially if you notice any gaps that need filling. Our local nursery carries plenty of primroses and winter pansies that are sure to bring a bit of joy to the garden in the quieter months, as well as winter lettuces and broad beans for the edible garden.

SOWING MONTH	FOOD	FLOWERS AND NON-EDIBLE SOWINGS
● September	· Chard · Kale · Land cress · Pak choi · Lettuce · Spinach · Dill · Mizuna (Japanese greens)	· Sweet peas · Foxgloves · Aquilegia (columbine) · Calendula · Cornflowers · Annual poppies · Wildflower mixes
● October	· Garlic · Onions · Shallots · Peas (hardy varieties)	· Violas and pansies · Lunaria (honesty)
● November	· Broad beans · Winter lettuce (under cover)	· –

I sow most of my edible autumn seeds in our polytunnel, mainly because that's where I have the most usable space that isn't already taken up with perennial crops. The benefit of polytunnel growing through autumn and winter is that our crops are slightly insulated from the harsher weather, suffer less damage from slugs where conditions are drier, and will grow a little earlier thanks to the warmer **microclimate**. However, all of these plants can be grown outdoors, with the exception of November-sown winter lettuce, which would struggle to germinate in cold conditions.

Growing in pots

All of these seeds and bulbs can also be grown in pots, making them a versatile option for gardeners with limited space or those who prefer container gardening. Aquilegias, known for their beautiful, delicate flowers, do have deeper taproots compared to many other plants. Therefore, they require taller pots to accommodate their root growth, ensuring healthy development and blooming. A pot that is at least 30–38cm (12–15in) deep would be ideal for aquilegias.

Cress, salads and herbs are particularly well-suited to growing in windowsill pots due to their relatively shallow root systems. These plants generally do not require deep soil to thrive, making them excellent choices for small containers or even shallow trays. This makes them accessible for indoor gardening, providing fresh greens close at hand. When growing these plants in pots, ensure good drainage by using pots with drainage holes and possibly adding a layer of gravel at the bottom. Regular watering is crucial, especially since containers can dry out quickly.

GARDEN JOBS FOR AUTUMN

In the fruit and vegetable garden:

- Harvest early autumn crops such as apples, pears, figs, autumn-fruiting raspberries, carrots, beetroot, chard, pumpkins and Brussels sprouts.

- Planting garlic cloves or bulbils is essential as they need the cold period of winter to develop into full bulbs by the summer.

- Sowing broad beans now will give them a head start for early spring harvests (see page 190).

- Weeding is crucial to prepare the beds for winter and to ensure that overwintering crops and bulbs have the best start without competition.

- Sowing green manure in empty plots can improve soil structure and fertility for the next year's planting (see page 177).

In the flower border:

- Planting bulbs for spring flowering, like daffodils, tulips and crocuses, is an autumn task that promises bursts of early colour next year (see page 158).

- Sowing hardy annuals such as strawflowers or sweet peas allows them to establish over winter, ready to bloom early in the spring.

- Cutting back some perennials helps tidy the garden, though it is vital to leave some stems and seedheads intact for wildlife shelter and food (see page 178).

- Making leaf mulch from fallen leaves enriches the soil and provides an excellent resource for next year's planting. Leaves can be removed and placed in a compost bin where they will break down, or left in situ on beds and borders to break down naturally (see page 175).

General garden care:

- Build hibernation spots for wildlife, such as hedgehog houses, and leave areas undisturbed for creatures to shelter over the winter months (see page 177).

- Top up bird feeders to support birds through the colder months when food is scarce (see page 178).

- Growing mushrooms in logs introduces a fascinating and productive element to the garden or woodland area, providing both an edible crop and an interesting project. Spore plugs can be purchased online, which should be drilled into stacks of logs and sealed with beeswax.

- Adding hedgehog houses in quiet, undisturbed parts of the garden encourages these beneficial mammals to take up residence and help control slugs and snails (see page 177).

- Mulch the soil with homemade compost to enrich soil fertility and structure without disturbing the soil layers, consistent with a no-dig approach. Ensure that there are no exposed patches of soil, which helps to protect the soil life, retain moisture and suppress weed growth over the winter months.

Observation:

- The change of season brings a shift in the garden's atmosphere and tasks. Embrace this transition by observing the changing colours, the wildlife preparing for winter, and the slow quieting of the garden.

- Enjoy the cooler days and the unique beauty of autumn in the garden. It's a time to prepare the garden and yourself for winter, but also to take stock and appreciate the cycle of growth and rest that defines gardening.

Above: planting tulip bulbs in a small cut flower bed. Opposite: top left, a shallow planting depth for non-perennial tulip bulbs; top right, an assortment of crocus and allium bulbs for autumn planting; bottom left, planting garlic cloves with a small bulb planter; bottom right, harvesting pears from the orchard.

W I
N

T　　E
　　　　R

Winter invites us to slow down.

The most beautiful winter mornings greet us with shimmering frost on the grass and an ethereal fog in the air. When I look out of the window and spot one of these particular mornings, I usher the dogs on an early walk through the village, following the downward slope of the valley towards the river, where the fog lasts all day. I watch the diffused sunlight as it attempts to break through the haze, while the dogs prance around on the crunchy frozen grass. If you time the walk early enough, the ground frost prevents the dogs from gathering their usual coating of winter mud too, and we are all grateful for avoiding their usual appointment with the shower. On my return from the walk, I will check on our garden, where our oak, plum and acer trees stand bare through the elements. Cobwebs delicately strung between branches are decorated with tiny droplets of dew, and wild creatures hibernate among their fallen leaves in the understory below. A little rummage through the natural mulch will reveal curled-up overwintering caterpillars and sleeping ladybirds, though I try to keep disturbance to a minimum. I welcome winter in our garden as an invitation to check in on my energy levels as the daylight hours lessen. Most of the garden falls into dormancy. The quiet is a reminder that rest is an essential part of life. The garden gives us permission to slow down.

I see the stripped-back garden as a blank canvas for us to reflect on. It is easiest to have a beautiful garden through summer, when colourful shrubs and perennials attract a viewer's attention with their immediate allure. The real challenge is whether a garden can still captivate you through winter.

Appreciating the beauty in winter relies on attention to detail – noticing the delicate structures of moss and lichen that decorate exposed branches, or the pale blue of the sky reflected on a frozen pond. There is an art of landscaping the garden in a way that inspires a viewer even before the space is filled with colourful perennials.

Evergreen trees and shrubs, favoured ornaments and rose branches pruned into interesting shapes can all provide beauty in these colder, more monochrome months.

The first few winters in my cottage garden were a bit of a reality check for me, because my planting and design efforts had so far centred heavily on what bloomed and thrived in the warmer months. We lacked evergreens in the backbone of our planting. So, I began building up a stock of plants that would bring little pops of colour and form through the colder months of the year.

Even the smallest of hellebores can provide so much inspiration in the absence of other flowers. I try to introduce varieties of hellebore that will flower as early as November. These flowers bring me such a sense of hope, both within their own beauty and as a broader reminder that the main flowering season will return again soon.

Creating an evergreen hedge

Gardening through winter has also taught me the value of an evergreen hedge. They provide an essential structure in the garden, as well as a habitat for wildlife. In springtime, I introduced pittosporum standards and Japanese holly domes to my flower borders for the valuable stature they provide when winter arrives, and I am gradually replacing many of my wooden fences with native yew hedging. I introduce the yew hedges as bare-root plants at the beginning of spring. Bare-root plants are lifted straight from their growing site during the dormant season and are more cost-effective than purchasing container-grown plants. With the funds saved by opting for bare-root plants, I select larger specimens, around 150cm (5ft) tall, helping them to look more established. These hedges are much more pleasing to look at than the wooden fences that stood before them, and because yew has an incredible potential lifespan of hundreds, if not thousands, of years, they should provide a boundary structure to the garden well beyond the scope of our own lifetimes. These evergreen hedges provide a soft, natural background in all other seasons, and in winter they stand strong as the heroes of the garden.

Feathered friends

For our flock of ducks, this is their quiet season too. In the UK, poultry are often required to be kept in an enclosure through winter to prevent the spread of avian flu, a process known by smallholders as 'flockdown'. Through the coldest weeks of the year, our ducks prefer to rest in the comfort of their barn anyway and don't seem to mind that it's compulsory, at least not for the first few months. While the ducks are confined to their enclosure I still try to give them enrichment in the form of kale, chard or squash, if we have any going spare. They are also grateful to go bobbing for peas in a bucket of water.

Runner ducks are surprisingly cold-hardy creatures, and during the winters when flockdown isn't enforced, it is quite entertaining to take them for a walk on the frozen pond, or an outing through the snowy orchard. They walk very politely across the snow-covered ground in their perfectly formed line, making tiny webbed footprints behind them.

It is rare for us to receive any duck eggs through winter, so our diets are instead built around stored vegetables like squash and potato, overwintering brassicas, or preserved fruits including tomatoes. I grow plenty of cavolo nero kale throughout the winter because I appreciate both its ornamental value and its flavour when harvested. One of my favourite recipes to prepare with freshly picked cavolo nero is a pot of Tuscan-style ribollita. Ribollita is a vegetable soup consisting of onions, carrots, celery, cannellini beans and cavolo nero, thickened with crusty bread. The name 'ribollita' translates to 'reboiled'. It has become a tradition for me to make a large pot of it on the hob and then reheat any leftovers for lunch the following day. Not only does it make for a wonderful comfort meal on a cold afternoon, in my opinion it tastes even better after the flavours have had a day to infuse.

Wildlife friendly Bundled up warmly, we enjoy a tea break outdoors, which offers a moment to observe birds feasting on berries, rosehips and uncleared growth. The robins in our garden are especially friendly, and last winter one was comfortable enough to land on my shoulder while I was sitting in the garden. The robins in our winter garden are kept company by blackbirds, goldfinches, and both great spotted and green woodpeckers, among a variety of birds. The green woodpeckers can be spotted foraging among the grass in the orchard. Usually, they notice me first and make a swift, flighty exit, giving me a chance to admire their colourful plumage as they fly away. The great spotted woodpeckers can be occasionally noticed in the canopy above as they cling to tree trunks. I don't notice the great spotted woodpeckers as often as their green counterparts, but the lack of leaves in winter makes it easier to spot them when they do pay us a visit.

I try to spend an hour or two outside every day in winter, even if the weather suggests otherwise. It makes a huge difference to my mood. I have invested in a thick pink snowsuit for the coldest of days, and some sturdy waterproofs and waders in case of rain. Daylight is scarce in winter here, with sunsets as early as 4pm on the shortest days. I make the most of every minute, and often find myself planting my leftover autumn bulbs in complete darkness with only a headtorch to guide me.

There are fewer garden tasks requiring our attention in winter. As gardeners we spend so much of our time looking forward, and while this gives me a valuable sense of hope and momentum, I have to remind myself to stop and appreciate my progress.

Winter is the time I like to work through each month in my notebook. I collate any notes I made in earlier seasons and look back through my camera roll for the year and ask myself: *what went well? What didn't? What did I learn, and what should I repeat next year?* More often than not I find myself positively overwhelmed by how full the year truly was, and through this I gain an appreciation for the necessity of winter rest.

Moments of rest and reflection

It can be difficult to find joy in short, cold days. But the falling temperatures have a vital role in the garden cycle, and I have learned to appreciate them. The frosts bring relief from pest populations and send a chemical message to our spring bulbs that initiates their growth once again.

Towards the end of this season, a glimpse of promise emerges as the earliest shoots push through the ground with new growth. A few flowering plants, such as hellebores and winter clematis, brave the season, later joined by the snowdrops, winter aconites and *Iris reticulata* that I planted in autumn; their delicate blooms are a welcome and reassuring sight.

As the winter solstice arrives, in December if you are in the northern hemisphere and June in the southern hemisphere, it feels like there's a collective celebration. We have made it through the shortest, darkest days. Brighter times are ahead.

Creating structure

After trees have dropped their leaves and our perennial plants retreat into a state of rest for winter, we are called to consider the structural features in our garden, such as bird baths, handmade plant supports or woven hazel fencing. These features may disappear into the background as flowers and leaves climb over them in summer, but through the barer seasons of winter into spring they keep a sense of charm alive.

Depending on how developed your garden already is, and whether you are happy with its current layout, winter is a good time to start to reconfigure your garden's design. This process may involve an element of hard landscaping or defining the space with fences, paths and hedges.

Although our garden was excessively overgrown when we moved in, underneath the masses of overgrowth were the bare bones of a cottage garden that someone had once loved. It was a case of cutting things back, ripping out invasive bamboo roots, digging out matts of neglected lily and crocosmia bulbs, and peeling back wild English ivy to reveal the foundations underneath.

Repairing existing structures

It took us a year to complete this removal stage. Afterwards, we began making repairs to underlying structures through the next winter and spring. With some help from friends and family, we re-sheeted a polytunnel frame with a new layer of plastic, replaced broken glass panes on two greenhouses, rebuilt a couple of small outbuildings and added a raised bed garden into the last empty patch of land. Each of these repairs expanded my options in the garden. The enclosed greenhouse meant I had a place to sow seeds with better protection from hungry birds and mice, the outbuildings gave us space to store tools, pots and even a freezer for preserving crops, and the raised beds became a home for my collection of edible perennial plants. We were on a very tight budget when we arrived, so I made our first two raised beds using thick pallet bearers that my father-in-law collected from a local pallet yard for free. I simply arranged the wooden bearers in a rectangle, and held them together with four corner brackets drilled inside. Conveniently, I also discovered that our local recycling centre

sold partially used tins of paint for a nominal price, so the total cost of the two raised beds was less than a single bag of compost, and one bed is painted in a pleasing shade of light turquoise.

I am someone who gets overwhelmed by demands quite easily, so it was important that we focused and worked through tasks one at a time, motivated by the idea of how each individual area we reinstated would allow us to garden in a new way. I try not to think of the bigger picture, and instead look right into the details so that things feel more achievable.

Our first task of putting the plastic sheet on the polytunnel frame gave me a warm and sheltered spot to grow melons and tomatoes the following summer, and through it, I gained a new bout of excitement that would gently move onto the next repair task when the growing season had finished.

A naturalistic garden

My style of gardening is naturalistic. This means a garden that mimics the natural world around it and makes space for native plants. In our garden, for example, we make space for the wild garlic that arrived naturally, most likely from the neighbouring woodland, and we embrace daisies, buttercups and cow parsley in the lawn. These plants naturally thrive here, as they are quite literally at home. They are adapted to our soil conditions and weather patterns, making them very easy to look after. A naturalistic garden also has an informal feel to it. Much like we observe in wild landscapes, the landscape of my garden eschews the rigid for the meandering, favouring curves and the use of reclaimed, natural materials to foster a sense of softness and continuity. Character comes from incorporating unique, weathered objects and from the thoughtful division of space with features like arches or naturalistic fencing, creating intimate 'rooms' within the garden.

Pathways

As a naturalistic garden style relies on reclaimed natural materials, pathways can be inexpensive and simple to make. A pathway will gently guide a viewer's eye towards focal points in your garden, and signpost a natural flow around the space. They are one of the easiest methods of creating a sense of layout within your garden, and opting for curves and meandering pathways over straight lines will help to create a friendly, informal feeling.

- The cheapest pathway is simply a mown pathway through long grass.

- For something more permanent but still affordable, you can lay stepping stones into your grass. This can be imprecise, with varying gaps between the stones, and if you sink the stones into the soil so that they are flush with the ground, you will be able to mow the lawn over them as normal. This is the approach we followed in our own garden. While we were restoring the flagstone floor in our cottage, we ended up with an assortment of broken flagstones that weren't usable in the house. The stones are a happy jumble of sizes and colours, and I sunk them into our lawn to create a natural pathway through the length of the whole garden.

- For a more prominent pathway, reclaimed bricks or flagstone laid closely together will be a more noticeable feature yet will still retain a timeless feel. You can make a feature of the gaps between paving stones by sowing perennial plants with dainty flowers, such as *Erigeron karvinskianus*, Roman chamomile or health pearlwort. *Erigeron* is one of my favourite plants for softening the edges of stone in our garden, and it self-seeds generously after you've added just one or two plants.

Greenhouses

Greenhouses and sheds make great focal points within a garden that you can frame your borders and pathways around. At the more expensive end of the scale, Victorian-style greenhouses built upon a dwarf brick wall are a timeless and beautiful asset to the garden. For those on a tighter budget, it is quite easy to come by free used greenhouse frames online (with or without glass panes), if you are willing to dismantle and rebuild them yourself. It will likely take a few days of effort and frustration, but will save a large amount of money and provide you with both a beautiful and practical addition to your garden.

We inherited two greenhouses when we moved into our home. The first was covered in such a large knot of brambles that it took us three months to notice it even existed. The second greenhouse, which is much larger than the first, deviates quite substantially from what you'd expect to see in a cottage garden. A previous owner had planted the greenhouse with an assortment of succulents and cacti, and although they weren't maintained over the years, the plants seem to have thrived on neglect. The greenhouse is sunken into the ground, and as you walk down the sandstone steps you are greeted by two huge agaves, each at least 1.2m (4ft) tall, and a collection of pricky pear cacti, too. When we first viewed the house, we were stunned by the presence and size of the agave plants, and even though they aren't a plant I would select for a cottage garden myself, we chose to preserve that playful sense of surprise by leaving them in place.

Sheds

When it comes to sheds, the easiest choice would be to find a flat-packed or pre-made shed and tuck it away in a corner. But sheds can also form an interesting focal point in your garden if you have the means to get creative. One possibility is to retrofit existing sheds with reclaimed timber windows and doors, and add a coat of colourful paint to create the appearance of a summerhouse. In our garden, a friend helped us build a shed from scratch that looks like a tiny grotto. He used reclaimed pantiles for the roof, and built bespoke arched windows around the edges. We had a mature elder tree that would have been in the way of the build, so rather than cut the tree down, our friend built the shed around the tree, so the tree grows through the inside of the shed and pops up out of the roof through its own little hatch. Our shed is unusual and quirky, and is now a favourite feature in the garden. It is proof that sheds don't need to be dull.

Arches and arbours

Arches and arbours are another garden structure that can be both useful and aesthetically pleasing. Arches can be used to train climbing flowers such as roses or clematis, and when the plants go dormant over winter, the arch will maintain the layout of your garden. Placing arches on the entrance or exit of garden rooms, or above central pathways, will help to create a natural flow around your growing space.

Arbours with seating underneath can also be used for climbing plants, but are best placed in a corner or along the edge of a fence or hedge so they blend into the landscape.

I installed two metal arches over the central pathway in our vegetable garden (see page 167), initially to guide the eye through the centre of the space. Over the years I have grown many interesting annuals over these arches, including pumpkins, climbing beans and the cup-and-saucer vine.

While growing these annuals I am patiently waiting for my permanent plants to become more established on the arches, which include a self-fertile kiwi 'Jenny', two climbing roses that I grew from cuttings and *Clematis* 'Piilu'.

Fencing

The type of fencing you use along the perimeter of your garden will likely be determined by your need for privacy, and safety for children or pets. Even if you are in need of tall fencing, there are still ways this can look natural.

In some parts of our garden we use pre-made hazel hurdles, which can be covered with climbing plants to create a living wall. The hurdles don't last very long, perhaps five or six years maximum, but they are incredibly beautiful and are very soft on the eye. Bespoke woven fencing has a much longer lifespan, but installation costs are much higher unless you learn to weave them yourself.

Currently, I am teaching myself how to weave willow fences and hurdles around the borders of beds and sections of the garden. Willow is harvested fresh through winter, so after I have collected the bunches from our local willow farm it is flexible enough to be woven with right away, rather than needing a period of soaking first.

If you are using shorter fences to divide your garden into separate sections, one option is picket fencing. Picket fencing is a simple but effective choice, and is easy to install yourself. If a picket fence feels too formal, a more natural choice is chestnut cleft fencing, which can be ordered pre-made as a roll.

The best choice for both keeping costs low and for creating a wildlife habitat is to create a 'dead hedge'. After installing vertical stakes, smaller woody branches and organic material cut from shrubs and trees is stuffed between the posts to create a barrier, to a height of your choosing. Dead hedges make wonderful homes for insects and birds, and can create feeding spots for mammals such as hedgehogs. We create very informal dead hedges at the end of our garden. I think of them as a nice transition between where our garden meets the wilderness.

Smaller ornaments

Some of the most characterful garden ornaments are those found second hand. One-of-a-kind objects that have been slightly weathered with age blend naturally into the garden and look like they have been there forever. We picked up two huge second-hand galvanised troughs from an old farmhouse, and after a difficult hour carrying them up a 300-foot slope into our garden, I filled them with 200 *Narcissus* 'Ice Follies' bulbs. Every spring the pale yellow flowers add a sign of life to the garden, and I appreciate the aged patina on the troughs, while the bulbs are dormant under the soil in winter.

Small garden ornaments come in a huge range of styles. There are classic garden ornaments such as bird baths or sundials, and there are more playful ornaments such as statues, sculptures, lanterns, watering cans, fountains – and gnomes. These smaller ornaments tend to be more affordable than other structural parts of the garden, and they give you a chance to express yourself, especially if you are creative or interested in art. In our garden, we have solar lanterns

hung up in tree branches through the length of the whole garden, which give us a sense of warmth in winter when the nights are long, and in summer we are often outside when the sun sets, and we just catch them lighting up as we transition into evening.

Some memorable ornaments observed in other people's gardens include a vintage bicycle with flowers growing in its basket, a rusty Victorian brass bedframe with a mini wildflower meadow planted within its frame, and a reclaimed ceramic toilet bowl filled with succulents.

I hope to one day recreate my grandma's collection of Beatrix Potter ornaments in our own garden. My grandma had a very steep slope in her garden, on which she built a rockery of heather plants. Nestled into the plants were stone ornaments of various characters, including Peter Rabbit and Mrs Tiggy-Winkle the hedgehog. When I was a young child Grandma would walk me into the garden and ask which characters I could spot on the hill. I know she enjoyed it just as much as I did, and though I probably won't go to the lengths of creating the full collection as my grandma did, I am currently on the lookout for a Jemima Puddle-Duck statue to place along the edge of my pond as a start.

Natural plant supports

A number of edible and ornamental plants require support to stop them toppling over in the growing season. While you can purchase simple metal plant supports from the garden centre, these do have a newness about them that can look out of place in a naturalistic garden. Experiment with making your own plant supports from materials such as bamboo, willow or hazel coppice (see image on page 86).

The easiest structures to make yourself are tripods or A-frames for climbing beans, roses or clematis:

- Sink three lengths of bamboo or hazel cane into your soil.

- Fasten together with wire at the top to create a tripod.

Flexible materials like willow can be used to weave shorter, more intricate supports for perennial plants, or even border edging and archways if you have enough material to use. We spent the best part of four years removing invasive bamboo from our garden, but the silver lining was the sheer volume of canes we gained to use in building small fences, plant supports and border edging.

A place to rest

It's worth planning a place to sit and admire your garden, to make the most of all the work you've invested in creating the space. Second-hand shopping is a great choice for finding ornate or natural seating – look for vintage wrought-iron bistro sets and wooden benches. I try to keep an eye on Facebook marketplace in particular for these kinds of purchases. Quite often when a homeowner is modernising their garden or having a clear out, they will want to get rid of anything old in favour of something brand new. We picked up a vintage two-seater bistro set for just £40 through Facebook marketplace. The seller couldn't understand why we were so excited about it, but it looks right at home in our cottage garden.

An ornate table set makes a pretty feature in a garden, but I would argue the act of stopping and sitting down is the most important thing here. I view my garden as a restorative place, and I have many days where the act of getting outside and doing the physical labour of gardening just isn't an option due to burnout or overwhelm. On those days, all I ask of myself is to get out there and sit or lie down, even if just for five minutes at the end of the day. There is no expectation to do anything or to plan future jobs. The garden might be weedy and the grass might want a tidy, but that doesn't matter. I just sit and watch things, or close my eyes and feel the texture of the grass.

My favourite place to sit is the step leading into my greenhouse. It's nothing fancy, but I treated myself to a waterproof cushion so I can sit and admire the view even during bad weather. The place I sit is directly opposite where the sun sets. I like to take up a cup of herbal tea and admire the way the colours change in the sky in that last hour of daylight.

As the garden transitions into dusk, tiny pipistrelle bats whizz around in circles, weaving through the trees and catching moths and other tiny insects. The simple act of watching them makes me feel a sense of wonder even on the most difficult of days. As a gardener it's easy to feel like your work is never done, but the garden should allow you to rest too, and that's where a comfortable place to sit is important.

COLOUR FOR COLD DAYS

Though there is only a small selection of winter-flowering plants to choose from when filling your garden, these plants hold immense value for the colour and joy they can inject into an otherwise quiet landscape. I find myself longing to see colourful blooms through the cold, grey months, and my hellebore collection is the perfect medicine for this when it comes into bloom at the end of winter. The display is also adored by the earliest pollinating visitors to the garden, who are in search of nectar when not an awful lot is available.

My winter garden doesn't bring the sense of abundance that is characteristic of spring or summer. It instead brings a sense of hope and strength via delicate flowers that emerge through the coldest and darkest of conditions, appearing to defy all odds.

Hellebores

I currently have around forty *Helleborus x hybridus* of various varieties in the garden, though I expect this number to creep up in successive years. Thanks to growing so many different types, there is a long flowering window that can begin as early as November (in a good year), and extend through to the end of April. Not all of the plants flower at once, so there is always a sense of intrigue as I wait for each remaining plant to join the parade. I was once lucky enough to find a variety of hellebore that flowered for ten months of the year, but in my excitement to share the plant I divided it a little too hastily and sadly lost it.

My most prized hellebore plants are my Evolution Group hellebores, which have been bred by hellebore specialists Ashwood Nurseries in Staffordshire. These hybrid hellebores have been curated to produce soft, sunset-coloured flowers, including yellows, peaches, apricots and reds. The flowers stand proudly upright compared to other varieties that can have a tendency to droop over, and the foliage of the plants is a distinctive yellow-green. Evolution hybrids are more expensive than other hellebores, but are a worthwhile treat if you are keen to build up a colourful winter garden. A few years ago, my mother-in-law and I took a trip to Ashwood Nurseries to see how the plants are bred and cared for, after which we chose a stunning yellow Evolution hellebore with rhubarb-pink stems for me to grow at home. I planted it as close to the house as possible, so I can admire its sunshine-coloured petals from the kitchen window on the gloomiest of winter days. Since then I have ordered a crowd of ten further Evolution hellebores to surround my beloved yellow plant, and it is a display that brings me so much comfort.

Growing the particularly pretty types of hellebore has ignited an interest in me for the more subtle varieties too, including our native variety, the 'stinking hellebore' or *Helleborus foetidus* (its common name is derived from the smell that is produced when the leaves are crushed), and the Corsican hellebore *Helleborus argutifolius*, which have simple lime green flowers, imposing upright structures, and dark green spiky or pointed leaves.

Hellebores are quite undemanding plants, and they prefer conditions like those on the edge of a woodland. They are best situated in light shade with some sun exposure, in enriched soil that won't become waterlogged. They can be grown in containers, but as they have large root systems it's worth giving them plenty of space. Like other perennials, it is best to plant hellebores outside of summer heat and drought. They are usually sold in nurseries throughout winter while they are in flower, and this timing means you can ensure you've chosen your preferred flower colour (in the other seasons hellebores are simply a mass of green or yellow foliage). When our garden is left to its own devices, many of the self-seeders are woodland plants – we have swathes of bluebells and wild garlic that grow larger every year, completely unassisted by me. It seems as though the garden naturally yearns for woodland-type plants, and so hellebores are quite happy here. Hellebores are my go-to plant for filling gaps in light or semi-shade. These gaps can feel more laborious to fill where they don't lend themselves naturally to showstopping and sun-loving blooms, and it sometimes feels like something of a compromise finding a suitable filler plant. Hellebores are a reward within themselves, and every winter I feel particularly grateful for their presence.

When it comes to upkeep, I feed our hellebores with a homemade liquid feed, usually comfrey and nettle, a couple of times in late spring or summer while the plants are producing new foliage, but after they have finished flower production. In the middle of winter I remove the old leaves, particularly if they look discoloured or unwell. This is mainly to improve the flower display, but can also assist in preventing the spread of disease. After a number of years in the ground the plants will become large enough to divide, and if you wish to multiply the plant it can be dug from the ground in autumn and partitioned through the middle using a spade and a knife.

It is possible to bring hellebores indoors for a vase, however my preference is to display the flowerheads floating in a large bowl of water on the table. Keeping the flowers upturned gives a better opportunity to appreciate the details in their unique colours and patterns, and the more varieties you introduce to the garden, the more captivating this display becomes.

Winter-flowering clematis

Other winter blooms in my cottage garden include winter-flowering clematis varieties 'Jingle Bells' and 'Freckles', which scramble through our woven hazel fencing and are adorned with nodding bell-shaped flowers in the winter months, and rich green foliage for the remainder of the year. My clematis plants are in partial shade against the hazel fencing, and they seem to get on quite happily. 'Freckles' tends to flower with speckled maroon petals at the start of winter, and is one of the only plants in the garden to do so intentionally (sometimes our roses produce a winter flush of flowers, but not reliably so). 'Jingle

Bells' flowers at the end of winter along with the hellebores, and has creamy white flowers. Both varieties produce evergreen foliage and are a great plant for year-round privacy.

Winter-flowering clematis require well-drained soil enriched with organic matter to support their growth and bloom. They should be planted in a location where they can receive morning sunlight and afternoon shade, as too much direct sun can stress the plants, especially during the summer. Support is crucial for these climbing plants; consider installing a trellis or hazel fencing to help guide their growth upward and prevent tangling. Pruning should be done sparingly, as these varieties bloom on the previous year's growth; trim lightly after flowering to maintain shape and health. An occasional feed of homemade liquid fertiliser or organic seaweed feed while the plant is putting on new growth will keep the plant healthy and encourage an abundance of flowers.

Iris reticulata

Towards the end of winter, you will find hundreds of *Iris reticulata* in flower in the borders of our garden, which I plant during my autumn bulb planting efforts. One of my favourite varieties is 'Katharine Hodgson', which produces tiny pale blue petals with a yellow centre, adorned with darker blue veins and spots. The pattern is so delicate I always feel as though the flowers have been painted by hand. Though they are small plants of about 12cm (4in) in height, I have found them to spread into clumps quite confidently, and over the years the displays have become much denser. Other varieties of *Iris reticulata* I grow include 'Frozen Planet' and 'Scent-Sational'.

To cultivate *Iris reticulata* effectively, select a sunny site with well-drained soil, as these bulbs are susceptible to rot in wet conditions. Plant the bulbs in late summer or early autumn, positioning them about 8–10cm (3–4in) deep and spaced approximately 7–10cm (3–4in) apart to allow room for spreading. *Iris reticulata* prefers a slightly **acidic** to neutral soil pH. After flowering, allow the foliage to die back naturally; this helps the bulbs gather energy for the next blooming season. Consider lifting and dividing the clumps every three to four years to rejuvenate vigorous growth and prevent vercrowding. This practice also gives you an opportunity to expand their presence in your garden or share them with fellow garden enthusiasts.

Snowdrops

Snowdrops are a small but powerful symbol of hope in the garden, persevering through cold temperatures and frozen earth to emerge as a mass of nodding white flowers at the start of February. There are hundreds of named cultivars of snowdrop (*Galanthus*), and those who are especially keen on the plants are known within the gardening community as 'galanthophiles'. Though I don't yet identify as a galanthophile myself, I am deeply fond of snowdrops and motivate myself through the darkest days of winter by making plans to visit snowdrop woodlands with my family in the weeks ahead.

I started planting snowdrops during my autumn bulb planting efforts three years ago, so I am still in the early stages of introducing them to the garden. My aim is to populate the space below my hellebore collection with the common snowdrop, *G. nivalis*. I have also planted a couple of thousand bulbs of *G. woronowii* in the grass where I grow my mini meadow, with the intention of extending the flowering season of the meadow so that it begins in winter and builds up towards the main flowering season in spring. Over time, these snowdrops should multiply and spread naturally by seed and division, and after they have flowered, I give them a helping hand by dividing the clumps of bulbs and replanting them in separate groups so that next year they cover an even broader area. Even though it has only been a few years, I am already impressed by the coverage of the snowdrops, and they give me a valuable sense of excitement for winter that I previously lacked.

Planting snowdrops is straightforward, making them an excellent choice for beginners looking to add early spring interest to their gardens. For best results, choose a location that mimics their natural woodland habitat: dappled shade under deciduous trees or shrubs is ideal. They prefer rich, well-drained soil that stays moist but not waterlogged. Plant the bulbs in the autumn, about 7–10cm (3–4in) deep and 5–7cm (2–3in) apart; this allows room for natural spreading. If you're planting a small number of bulbs in grass, as with a mini meadow, simply push each bulb into the soil using a dibber or similar tool, and they will settle in without much disturbance to the area. For planting larger quantities in the grass, it may be more efficient to lift the turf with a spade and plant below (see page 162 for details).

Winter-flowering shrubs

I am in the process of introducing a few winter-flowering shrubs to our garden. Those that I have already planted have only been here for a few years and so are still quite small, but I feel assured that as I spend

my time tending to the garden around them, they will quietly grow into the foreground before I know it. I chose a camellia shrub with creamy white flowers and positioned this against the boundary fence so that in future years its evergreen foliage will enhance the privacy of the garden. We have already been rewarded with two flushes of winter blooms, despite the plant being so young.

Camellias are **ericaceous** plants and so prefer to grow in acidic soil, though neutral soil is also tolerable. For the most part, our soil is neutral or leaning slightly towards alkaline, so I use an ericaceous liquid plant food and oak leaves on the soil surface to adjust the acidity slightly. Camellias prefer partial sun, and their ideal placement is where they can be protected from the early morning sun, which can damage the flowers and leaves if they are frosted.

Daphne odora is next on my 'to plant' list for winter colour. Once I get round to sourcing one, it should provide us with highly scented clusters of pale pink flowers in midwinter, and deep green foliage all year round. Other winter-flowering shrubs to consider growing include witch hazel (*Hamamelis*), which dazzles with its spidery yellow to red flowers and aromatic scent; mahonia, known for its bright yellow racemes that add a burst of sunshine to the dreary winter landscape; and viburnum, particularly *Viburnum x bodnantense*, which produces pink to white fragrant flowers even on the coldest days.

Seeking inspiration and reflecting on the year

When I am out in the garden, I can disappear for an entire afternoon with great ease. On my return to the house, my partner will ask, 'What did you get up to out there today?', and often I have no idea. I can become so engrossed in the process of gardening that it doesn't feel conscious. One task will invariably lead into another, and then another, and then another, and in no time at all, six hours have elapsed and I've meandered through a multitude of unplanned tasks. I like to work so that the garden leads me, rather than going out with a strong objective. I feel like the garden can carry me into its own magical world this way, and I also think we owe it to our gardens to let them lead.

One action that I do enforce, though, is note-taking. I try to unplug while I'm outdoors, but I have found the notes app on my phone to be somewhat of an essential tool. I have a note for plant names and planting locations, a list of perennials I would like to plant, a list of areas that could use some care or attention, a list of bulbs I have planted (and how I felt about them on seeing them flower), a list of bulbs I would like to plant and why the conditions of certain areas meet the needs of those bulbs, and the list goes on. My notes app is inspired, jumbled and sprawling – much like a happy and healthy garden.

To accompany my notes, there are hundreds of photos. I try to take an assortment of quick photos every week or so for documentation purposes. There is no expectation to share these with anyone beyond myself. There is just the notion that when winter arrives it will feel reassuring to look back at the beauty of warmer and greener days. I use my phone for this because it is usually available, and it organises photos very clearly by months or years, and so in times of reflection, the relevant photos are always easily accessible.

When winter arrives, I make an effort to reflect through my notes and photos. It has become an annual ritual.

For my winter reflections, I move from my phone to pen and paper. There is something about the solidity of writing by hand that feels concrete and official, which my excited but hastily written phone notes lack. My winter reflection feels like it completes the yearly cycle. I devote a page of the notebook to each month of the year and consider the following:

- What looked beautiful?

- Did we see any wildlife, and was this different to last year?

- What didn't work, and what did we learn from that?

- What do we want to see in this month next year, and how can we plan for that?

- What did my life look like outside of the garden, and how did this affect how I gardened?

- Did I visit any other gardens or areas of natural beauty this month, and if so, did I bring any information or plants home with me?

After working through those details, you can start to ask questions about the garden year as a whole, or the bigger picture entirely:

- What really stood out this year?

- What felt hard and why?

- Was there anything I completely forgot about, and was this a problem?

- Did the things I learned or felt interested in fall under a particular title, and what was it?

Reflecting in this way may sound obvious or simple, and potentially even somewhat patronising, but actually partaking in it feels expansive and exciting. You might want to dedicate a fresh notebook for these reflections, but I've included some pages overleaf to help you get started.

In my gardening journey so far, I have noticed themes of each particular year. In the earliest months of that first year of gardening, I was building up foundational knowledge of how to sow seeds, how to plant, how to prune and so on. I was learning the conventional gardening wisdom, and through practice beginning to understand which parts were useful to me, and which parts less so.

As the years went on, I had the time to become more interested in particular planting niches – the different species of tulips, trends in gardens over time, wild gardens, polycultures. Then beyond practicalities, I also noticed the smaller details and glimmers that had brought me a sense of deep wonder. Last year, for example, I noticed how light varies in colour and intensity throughout the course of a day, and how this changes through the year. At the end of last summer we had our wildlife pond relined and refilled, and I sat on a railway sleeper opposite the water for three uninterrupted hours watching the newts, frogs and dragonflies arriving to their new home. It was such a simple thing, but it felt so rewarding.

This year I can't take my eyes off the trees, and I am engrossed by how the shades of green change through their growth cycle. I have also never seen so many ladybirds as I have this year, and so in terms of wild gardening and encouraging natural predation, we must be doing something right.

The point is, though, these details are what gardening is about. With a bit of intentionality and time, which the season of winter kindly gifts to us, we can reflect and feel proud of the depth in our journey so far, and wildly excited for the next chapter.

SPRING REFLECTIONS

In spring I planted...

Wildlife I noticed...

Plants that inspired me...

SUMMER REFLECTIONS

In summer I harvested…

I grew from seed…

One highlight included…

AUTUMN REFLECTIONS

In autumn I enjoyed...

Wildlife I encouraged...

Changes I spotted...

WINTER REFLECTIONS

In winter I noticed…

One thing I have learned is…

Next year I will…

GARDEN JOBS FOR WINTER

In the edible garden:

- Prune apple trees – winter is the ideal time to prune apple trees as they are dormant during this period. Pruning helps to open up the tree canopy, allowing sunlight and air to reach the inner branches, and encourages healthy growth and fruit production in the coming season.

- Protect vulnerable plants with fleece or other insulating materials if frost is forecast. Covering plants with protective materials helps to shield them from frost damage. This is particularly important for young plants and tender perennials, which can be severely impacted by sudden temperature drops.

In the flower border:

- Clear away growth on perennials that will turn soft and mushy, and leave growth that will provide seedheads for feeding birds or hibernation spots for insects. Remove decayed and overripe plant material to prevent diseases and pests from harbouring over winter. However, leaving some dead stems and seedheads provides food for birds and shelter for hibernating insects, enhancing biodiversity.

- Evaluate the layout and health of evergreen plants, which act as the backbone of the winter garden by providing structure and colour. Consider adding or replacing evergreens to improve year-round interest in the garden.

- Remove old foliage from hellebores before they flower. Cleaning up old, dead leaves from hellebores not only tidies up the plant but also reduces the risk of disease and pest infestation. This helps ensure the flowers are visible and healthy as they bloom in late winter or early spring (see page 225).

General garden care:

- Move leaves from lawn onto borders, and leave intact on the soil for the most wildlife and soil-friendly approach. A natural leaf mulch conserves moisture and improves soil structure. Decomposing leaves also attract wildlife, such as worms and beneficial insects, which help to aerate the soil and break down organic matter. If a tidier garden is desired, leaf mulch can be made by collecting leaves in a compost bin or large bag (see page 175).

- Clean algae from greenhouses or polytunnels. Algae can block light and harbour pests and diseases. Cleaning it from the structures ensures that your plants receive maximum light and reduces the potential for problems.

- Make structural repairs while plants have died back. Winter is a good time to fix fences, trellises and other garden structures. With plants dormant and garden beds bare, it is easier to access and repair any damage without harming your plants.

- Evergreens and newly planted trees and shrubs may need additional water during dry spells in the winter, especially if the weather is windy or sunny.

- Winter can be a challenging time for birds in terms of finding food. Keeping bird feeders stocked with a variety of seeds, suet and nuts helps sustain bird populations when natural food sources are scarce (see page 178).

Observation:

- Take time to appreciate the beauty of frost-covered plants and the quiet of a winter garden. These moments can offer peace and a different perspective on your garden's seasonal changes.

- Reflect on the year and make plans for next year in the garden. Use the downtime winter provides to think about what worked and what didn't over the past year. Planning for the next year can involve rotating crops, introducing new plants, or redesigning parts of the garden.

- Plan next year's seed list. Winter is the perfect time to order seeds for the upcoming planting season. Researching plants and planning your seed purchases can ensure you get the varieties you want and are prepared when it's time to start seeds indoors or plant outside.

GARDENING IN A DIFFERENT CLIMATE

I live in Somerset, in the south-west of England, and my guidance is based on working in that climate. If you are in a different part of the world, you might want to consult the RHS guide to **hardiness ratings**, to see how your climate compares (I am in RHS zone H4/USDA zone 9a). Access it here: rhs.org.uk/advice/rhs-hardiness-rating

Gardening seasonal conversion chart

For a quick reference on what each month of the year means for your climate, you can consult the table opposite.

NORTHERN HEMISPHERE (E.G. UK, EUROPE, US)	MONTH	SOUTHERN HEMISPHERE (E.G. AUSTRALIA)
● Winter	January	● Summer
● Winter	February	● Summer
● Spring	March	● Autumn
● Spring	April	● Autumn
● Spring	May	● Autumn
● Summer	June	● Winter
● Summer	July	● Winter
● Summer	August	● Winter
● Autumn	September	● Spring
● Autumn	October	● Spring
● Autumn	November	● Spring
● Winter	December	● Summer

Glossary

GENERAL GROWING TERMS

Annual
Plants that complete their entire lifecycle, from germination to the production of seeds, within one year, and then die.

Biennial
Plants that complete their lifecycle over two years, typically flowering in the second year.

Hardiness Zone
A geographic area defined by its climatic conditions, particularly its cold tolerance, helping gardeners determine which plants are most likely to thrive at their location.

Hungry Gap
The period in spring when winter crops have finished but early summer crops are not yet ready to harvest.

Perennial
Plants that live for more than two years, often blooming each season once they reach maturity.

GARDEN PLANNING AND LAYOUT

Full Shade
Areas that receive little to no direct sunlight, suitable for plants that can thrive with minimal light.

Full Sun
Refers to areas that receive direct sunlight for at least six to eight hours per day, ideal for plants that thrive in lots of light.

Microclimate
The climate of a small, specific area within a garden that can be different from the overall climate of the region. Factors such as walls, water bodies, and plant density can create microclimates.

Partial Shade
Areas that are shaded for part of the day or receive filtered sunlight, suitable for plants that need protection from intense midday sun.

SOIL COMPOSITION AND HEALTH

Acidic
Soil with a pH value below 7.0, characterised by its ability to support the growth of plants that thrive in low pH conditions, such as blueberries and rhododendrons.

Ericaceous
Refers to plants that thrive in acidic soil conditions. These plants often require soil with a pH of less than 7 and are typically included in the rhododendron and azalea family.

Mulching
Applying a layer of material on the surface of the soil to conserve moisture, improve fertility, and reduce weed growth.

Nitrogen, Phosphorus, Potassium (NPK)
The three major nutrients required by plants, often listed on fertiliser packages. Nitrogen promotes leaf growth, phosphorus is important for root and flower development and potassium is crucial for overall plant health.

METHODS OF GARDENING

Companion Planting
A type of polyculture, in which particular species of plants are grown together in the interest of deterring pests, attracting pollinators or utilising a space to the fullest extent.

No Dig
A gardening method that involves minimal soil disturbance, maintaining soil structure and health by adding compost and other organic matter on top of the soil rather than digging.

Organic
A method of gardening that relies on natural processes and materials to grow plants, avoiding synthetic chemicals for pest control or fertilisation.

Permaculture
A philosophy of gardening that mimics the natural ecosystems, creating sustainable and self-sufficient agricultural environments.

Polyculture
Growing multiple types of plants together in the same space to mimic natural ecosystems, improving diversity and resilience. This methodology is opposed to monoculture or monocropping.

PLANT DESCRIPTORS

Deciduous
Plants that shed all their leaves for part of the year, typically in autumn.

Evergreen
Plants that retain their leaves throughout the year, providing continuous foliage.

Hardy
A plant that is able to tolerate sub-zero temperatures (though there is variation between hardy plants in just how cold they are able to tolerate).

Invasive Plant
Non-native plants that spread aggressively, outcompeting local flora and potentially causing environmental harm.

Native Plant
Plants that occur naturally in a particular region or ecosystem without human introduction.

Naturalised Plants
Non-native plants that adapt to a new area and grow as if they were native, often spreading beyond the garden.

Non-native Plant
Plants that have been introduced to an area where they do not naturally occur.

Self-fertile
Plants that can pollinate themselves and do not require a different variety to produce fruit.

Tender
Plants that will not survive a frost.

Variegated
Plants that have leaves containing multiple colours. These colours can appear in blotches, stripes or edges, often making the plants highly decorative.

SEED SOWING

Compost
Decomposed organic material used as a soil amendment for plant growth.

Hardening Off
Gradually acclimatising indoor or greenhouse-grown plants to outdoor conditions to prevent shock.

Last Frost Date
The average date of the last expected frost in spring, guiding gardeners on when it is safe to plant frost-sensitive seeds and seedlings outdoors.

Modules
Small compartments or cells in a tray used for sowing individual seeds or small groups of seeds.

Potting On
The process of transferring seedlings to a larger pot to encourage continued growth before transplanting them into the garden.

Pricking Out
The process of transplanting seedlings from their initial growing medium to individual pots or modules, allowing them more space to grow.

Propagator
A device or container used to create optimal growing conditions for seeds and cuttings, often providing controlled temperature and humidity to encourage germination.

Seedling
A young plant that has recently emerged from a seed.

Thinning Out
The practice of removing some plants, or parts of plants, to allow more space for the remaining plants to grow. This is commonly done with seedlings to prevent overcrowding.

True Leaves
The first set of leaves that resemble the plant's mature leaf form, following the initial simpler seed leaves.

Vermiculite
A mineral mixed with soil or compost to improve aeration and moisture retention, aiding seedling development.

PLANT CARE

Coppicing
A traditional method of woodland management that involves periodically cutting trees and shrubs to ground level to stimulate growth.

Deadheading
The process of removing spent flowers from plants. This is often done to maintain a plant's appearance, encourage further blooming, or prevent seed production that can drain a plant's energy.

Pruning
Cutting back parts of a plant to improve its shape, encourage growth or maintain its health. Pruning can involve removing dead or diseased wood, thinning the crown to increase airflow, or shaping the plant for design purposes.

Seaweed or Comfrey Fertiliser
Organic fertilisers made from seaweed or comfrey plants, used to provide nutrients to plants.

Supports
Structures such as stakes, trellises or nets used to support the growth of climbing or tall plants, preventing them from falling over.

Topiary
The art of clipping trees and shrubs into ornamental shapes.

Index

A
agastache 188
algae 243
annuals 112, 115, 116, 191, 196
apple trees 69, 242
aquatic plants 51, 52
aquilegias 194
arches and arbours 216, 219
artichokes, globe 123
Ashwood Nurseries 225
asparagus 119, 132, 144, 178
asters 187–8
autumn 142–99, 240
avian flu 107, 147, 205

B
bamboo 221
basil 28, 132
bats 50, 90, 93, 94, 131, 177, 222
bay 73, 77
beans 56, 132, 178, 219
    broad beans 35, 84, 94, 138, 177, 190–1, 196
    French beans 134, 138
bees 40, 44, 131
biodiversity, encouraging 85
bird baths 131, 210, 220
birds 50–1, 94, 131, 147, 206
    feeding 178, 181, 197, 243
blueberries 94, 138, 144
borders, planting 64–7
box 70, 73
box tree caterpillars 70, 73
brain fireworks 40–4
broad beans 35, 84, 94, 138, 177, 190–1, 196
brown waste 139
bulbs 43, 209
    everlasting tulips 32, 35, 85, 168–72
    lifting and dividing 166
    meadow upkeep 165–6
    naturalised bulbs 48, 85, 152–7, 158–61
    planting 148, 152–67, 172, 196
    planting in lawns 162–3
    planting in pots 164
    protecting from pests 165
    reasons to plant 158
    when to plant 162
    see also individual plant species
bumblefoot 107

C
calendula 132
camellia 77, 233
carbon capture 46, 112
caterpillars 70, 73, 115, 126, 132, 175, 202
cauliflower 134
cavolo nero kale 190, 206
chamomile, Roman 124
chard 190, 205
chilli powder 165
chives 124
clematis 35, 82, 85, 178, 209, 216, 219
    winter-flowering 81, 226, 229
climate: climate change 46, 112
    gardening in different climates 246–7
climbing plants 35, 81–2, 216, 219
cold frames 56, 61
collards 119
collared doves 50–1
comfrey plant food 48, 85, 93, 128, 138, 172, 226
companion planting 94, 131–2
compost 56, 61, 84, 93, 127, 138, 139
    duck compost 100, 103
compost bins 90, 127, 177, 196
cornflowers 191
The Courts Garden, Wiltshire 152
covering plants 242
creeping buttercups 183
crocuses 40
    choosing bulbs 159, 160
    crocus lawns 20, 44, 48, 74, 85, 152, 156, 159
    food source for pollinators 66–7
    planting 158, 162, 164, 196
    saffron crocuses 144, 147, 187
cutting back 85, 178, 196

D
daffodils (*Narcissus*) 160, 164, 165, 196, 220
    naturalised 35, 156, 159, 162, 166
damsons 69, 94, 138, 175
Daphne odora 233
Daubenton's kale 119
David Austin roses 64, 66, 74, 77
dead hedges 219
deadheading 85, 138
diseases 139
doves, collared 50–1
ducks 32, 90, 93, 147–8
    bumblefoot and flu 107
    choosing your flock 104
    compost 100, 103
    diet 108
    eggs 99, 147, 206
    gender ratio 104
    housing 108
    joy of companionship 103
    life span 107
    mud and mess 106
    as pest control 100
    potential predators 106, 108
    runner ducks 96–109, 205–6
    space to roam 108
    tips 104–7
    vermin and 107
    water 108

E

echinacea 78, 178, 183, 184
edible plants 36, 54, 132, 144
    perennials 112–25
    planting edible bulbs 172
    sowing seeds in autumn 190–1
Erigeron karvinskianus 78, 81, 93, 215
evergreens 70, 77, 204, 205, 242
everlasting onions 120

F

feeding plants: comfrey plant food 48, 85, 93, 128, 131, 138, 172, 226
    in summer 93–4
fencing 210, 219, 243
figs 69, 70, 73
fleece 242
flowers: autumn flowers 182–9, 196
    flower-rich meadows 46
    flowering edibles 132
    introducing new 64–7
    sowing seeds 134
    spring jobs 85
    summer jobs 138–9
    winter flowers 224–33, 242
flu, avian 107, 147, 205
foxes 106, 126
foxgloves 78, 93, 134
French beans 134, 138
frogs 50, 51, 90, 94, 100, 126, 147, 177, 237
frost 62, 64, 84, 175, 202, 209, 242
fruit: autumn jobs 196
    fruit trees 69–70, 85, 94, 116, 242
    harvesting 138, 144, 196
    perennial 123–4
    spring jobs 84
    summer jobs 138

G

gardening practices, impact of 29
garlic 138, 172, 196
geraniums, hardy 78
glimmers, finding 40–4
globe artichokes 123
grapes 82
grass clippings 27, 66, 93, 127, 138, 139
green manure, sowing 177–8, 196
greenhouses 56, 61, 100, 210, 215–16, 222
    cleaning 243

H

habitat conservation 131
hard landscaping 210
hardening off 58, 61, 84
hardy geraniums 78
hazel 69, 221
hedgehogs 126, 174, 177, 197
hedges 138, 205
dead hedges 219
    in spring 70–3
height, building up 73
Helianthus 'Lemon Queen' 184
hellebores 205, 209, 224, 225–6, 242
herbs, perennial 124
hibernation spots 177, 197
hostas 51, 178
Hydrangea 74
    H. 'Limelight' 184, 187

I

Iford Manor, Wiltshire 156
insects 85, 158, 175, 177, 181, 219, 242
    leaf mulch 242–3
invasive plants 67, 68
Iris reticulata 160, 209, 229
Iroquois 131–2
ivy 181

J

Japanese anemone 187
Jerusalem artichokes 123, 188

K

kale 115, 119, 132, 177, 190, 205, 206
kiwi vines 82, 116, 219

L

labels, plant 56
lasagne planting method 164
lawns 35, 85
    crocus lawns 20, 44, 48, 74, 85, 152, 156, 159
    embracing an untamed lawn 46–9
    meadows 152, 156, 159
    mowing 93, 139, 165
    naturalised bulbs 158–9, 162–3
leaves 148
    clearing up 242
    hibernation spots 177
    leaf mulch 175, 181, 196, 242–3
leeks, perennial 120
lighting 220–1
lilac 74
Linaria 78

M

mahonia 233
manure: duck manure 100, 103
    sowing green manure 177–8, 196
meadows 46, 85, 152, 156, 159
    bulb meadow upkeep 165–6
Mexican fleabane 78, 81, 93, 215
mint 124

mistakes, learning to love 28
moss 157, 164, 202
mulches and mulching 84
    autumn leaves 175
    conserving moisture with 66, 128, 138
    duck manure 103
    grass clippings 93
    living mulches 132
    natural mulches 127, 128, 148, 172
    and soil health 69, 197
mushrooms 197
mycorrhizal fungi 112

N

nasturtiums 132
native plants 66–7
naturalised bulbs 152–7, 158–61
naturalistic gardens 214, 215
nature, working with 126–33, 174–81
nettles 128, 138
newts 50, 51, 90, 93, 96, 100, 147, 177, 237
nitrogen 93, 103, 128, 132
    nitrogen fixing 134, 191
No Mow May 46, 48
No-Mow Movement 46, 48–9
non-native plants 66–7
note-taking 234, 236
nut trees 69, 70

O

observation 85, 139, 197, 243
onions 115, 120, 138, 172
orchids 48
oriental poppies 78, 85, 93
ornaments, smaller 220–1

P

parasitic wasps 126, 132
pathways 215
peas 56, 134, 138, 205
Penstemon 'Sour Grapes' 188
perennials 54, 85, 94
    autumn-flowering 183
    cutting back 178, 196, 242
    edible 112–25
    in spring 77–81
    in summer 112–25
pests 112
    bulbs and 165
    checking for 84, 139
    companion planting 124, 131, 132
    deterring 94, 124, 131, 132, 165
    frost and 209
    natural pest control 51, 73, 90, 100
    perennials and 115
    planting bulbs deep 171
    seedlings and 57, 58
    see also individual types of pest

phosphorus 103
photos 234
plant labels 56
Plantlife 46
plants, choosing 64, 66
pollinators 40, 126, 158
    apple trees and 69
    autumn-flowering plants 184, 188
    companion planting 131, 132
    crocuses and 66
    decline in food sources for 46
    encouraging 48, 49, 54, 66, 85, 191
    herbs and 124
    Mexican fleabane and 81
    roses 82
    weigela and 74
polycultures 27–8, 94, 131–2
polytunnels 56, 61, 194, 210, 213, 243
ponds 50–3, 90, 96, 131, 237
poppies, oriental 78, 85, 93
potassium 103, 128
potatoes 134, 206
pots 164, 194, 220
potting on 57–8, 61, 84
pricking out 84
pruning 85, 139, 242
purple tree collards 119

R

rainwater storage 128, 139
rats 107
rest and reflection, moments of 209
rhubarb 123
Roman chamomile 124
rosehips 178, 181
roses 93, 144, 204
    climbing 81, 82, 216, 219
    David Austin roses 64, 66, 74, 77
    deadheading 138
    mulching 103
    rosehips 178, 181, 206
    shrub roses 73, 74, 77
Rudbeckia 'Golsturm' 184
runner ducks 96–109, 205–6

S

saffron crocuses 144, 147, 187
seasonal conversion chart 246–7
seating 222
seed trays and modules 56, 61
seedlings: hardening off 58, 61, 84
    potting on 57–8, 61, 84
    pricking out 84
    thinning out 57, 61
seeds: green manure 178
    how to sow 56–8
    organising 84
    planning next year's seed list 243
    seed collecting 132
    seed sowing checklist 61

sowing 54–9, 61, 138, 190–5
watering 56, 61
what to sow in spring 62–3
sheds 216
shrubs: cutting back 178
evergreens 204
introducing new 64–7
pruning 85
in spring 73–7
topiary 70–3
watering 73–4, 243
winter-flowering 230, 233
sitting areas 222
slow worms 90, 126
slugs and snails 51, 56, 90, 100, 126, 127, 177, 194, 197
snake's head fritillaries 35, 48, 156, 157, 158, 159, 161
snowdrops 209, 230
choosing bulbs 158, 159, 160
lifting and dividing 166
naturalised plantings 85, 158, 159, 162
planting in pots 164
soil: mulches and mulching 127, 128, 197
soil health 27, 48, 100, 112, 134, 172
sowing: autumn sowing 190–5
green manure 177–8, 196
how to sow 56–8
seed sowing checklist 61
spring sowing 62–3
summer sowing 134–7, 138
spring 30–87, 238
squash 132, 138, 178, 205, 206
squirrels 69, 147, 163, 165, 177, 181, 187
strawberries 123–4, 144
structure, creating 210–23, 243
summer 88–141, 239
sunflowers 181, 184
supports, plant 78, 84, 85, 134, 210, 221
swede 134
sweet peas 191, 196
sweetcorn 132, 138

T

tables 222
taproots 48, 183
thinning out 57, 61
'Three Sisters' method 131–2
toads 90, 100, 177
tomatoes 54, 178, 206, 213
companion planting 132
feeding 94, 128
harvesting 94, 138, 144
mulching 127
pests and 132
seedlings 57
when to sow 63
topiary 70–3
toxicity 68
trees 64–7, 69–70, 204
pruning 139
topiary 70–3
watering 243

troughs 220
tulips 100, 148
choosing 161
growing everlasting 32, 35, 85, 168–72
pests and 165
planting 158, 164, 171, 196
post-flowering care 171–2

V

vegetables 54, 94
annuals 112, 128
autumn jobs 190, 196
feeding 128
harvesting 36, 138, 144, 196
perennials 112–23
spring jobs 84
summer jobs 138
see also individual types of vegetable
vermiculite 56, 61
viburnum 233

W

walking onions 120
wasps, parasitic 126, 132
watering 139
new plants 66
pots 194
rainwater storage 128, 139
seeds 56, 61
shrubs 73–4
in spring 66
in winter 243
weeds and weeding 138, 139, 183, 196
autumn weeding 183
making friends with weeds 48–9
suppressing weeds 127, 132
weigela 74, 144
whitefly 115, 132
wildlife 48
in autumn 147, 174, 175, 177
dead hedges 219
habitat conservation 131
hibernation spots for 177, 197
leaf mulch 242–3
ponds 50–3, 90, 96, 237
in summer 90–4
wildlife-friendly plants 66–7
working with nature 126, 131–2
see also individual species
willow 219, 221
winter 70, 73, 200–47
witch hazel 233
woodpeckers 206

Y

yew 70, 205

ACKNOWLEDGEMENTS

Thank you to my kind and gentle husband, Aaron, who created the photography for this book. It is such a privilege to build a life together and to celebrate it through our shared creative work.

I would like to express my deepest gratitude to my wonderful literary agent, Megan, who guided this book from concept to completion, and to Laura and Emily at Ebury, who helped bring my ideas to life. The three of you have been an incredibly supportive team, offering so much warmth and encouragement while allowing me to work within my limits.

Ebury Press, an imprint of Ebury Publishing, Penguin Random House UK
One Embassy Gardens, 8 Viaduct Gardens, Nine Elms, London SW11 7BW

Ebury Press is part of the Penguin Random House group of companies whose addresses can be found at global.penguinrandomhouse.com

Copyright © Ramona Jones 2025
Photography © Aaron Gibson and Ramona Jones 2025

Ramona Jones has asserted her right to be identified as the author of this Work in accordance with the Copyright, Designs and Patents Act 1988

First published by Ebury Press in 2025

www.penguin.co.uk

A CIP catalogue record for this book is available from the British Library

ISBN 9781529944303

Design by Sandra Zellmer
Colour origination by Altaimage Ltd
Printed and bound in China by
C&C Offset Printing Co., Ltd

Penguin Random House is committed to a sustainable future for our business, our readers and our planet. This book is made from Forest Stewardship Council® certified paper.

Penguin Random House values and supports copyright. Copyright fuels creativity, encourages diverse voices, promotes freedom of expression and supports a vibrant culture. Thank you for purchasing an authorized edition of this book and for respecting intellectual property laws by not reproducing, scanning or distributing any part of it by any means without permission. You are supporting authors and enabling Penguin Random House to continue to publish books for everyone. No part of this book may be used or reproduced in any manner for the purpose of training artificial intelligence technologies or systems. In accordance with Article 4(3) of the DSM Directive 2019/790, Penguin Random House expressly reserves this work from the text and data mining exception.